Autumn

Back to School

Native Americans

Christopher Columbus

Halloween

Thanksgiving

Seasonal Activities • EMC 2004 • © Evan-Moor Corp.

Name ―――――――――――――――

Name It

Fall is another name for **autumn**.
Write a word beginning with a letter in **fall** under each category.

	something in your house	a part of your body	a fruit or vegetable	a city or state	an animal with 4 legs
Example T	table	toe	turnip	Texas	turtle
F					
A					
L					
L					

  Seasonal Activities • EMC 2004 • © Evan-Moor Corp.

First Day of Autumn

Read the paragraph and then answer the questions.

In the Northern Hemisphere, the first day of autumn is usually September 22. (In the Southern Hemisphere, it is usually March 21.) It is one of two days each year when day and night are the same length. This is the beginning of shorter days and longer nights. The weather becomes cooler. It is a time to harvest many types of crops. It is time for animals to begin preparing for winter.

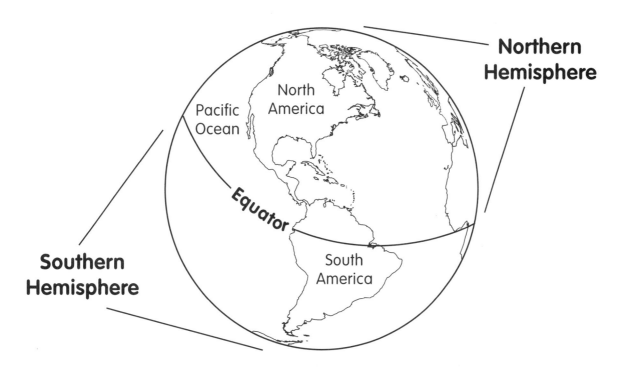

1. When is the first day of autumn in the Northern Hemisphere?

   _____

2. What types of changes occur during autumn? _____

   _____

3. Describe how an animal might prepare for winter.

   _____

   _____

Name _____

Autumn Crossword Puzzle

Use the clues to solve the crossword puzzle.

Seasonal Activities • EMC 2004 • © Evan-Moor Corp.

Across

2. the month in which autumn begins

3. a disguise worn on Halloween

4. the _____ begins to cool in autumn

6. what Columbus called the Native Americans

10. these fall from trees in autumn

11. one of the discoverers of America

13. the color of most pumpkins

15. special days of celebration

Down

1. the month in which Halloween occurs

2. a furry animal that collects nuts for winter

5. something tasty given out on Halloween

7. acorns and almonds are types of _____

8. the month after October

9. a special holiday in November

12. the night for trick-or-treating

14. another name for autumn

Word Box

Columbus	nuts
costume	October
fall	orange
Halloween	September
holidays	squirrel
Indians	Thanksgiving
leaves	treat
November	weather

Name _____

Autumn Colors

Read the paragraph and then answer the questions.

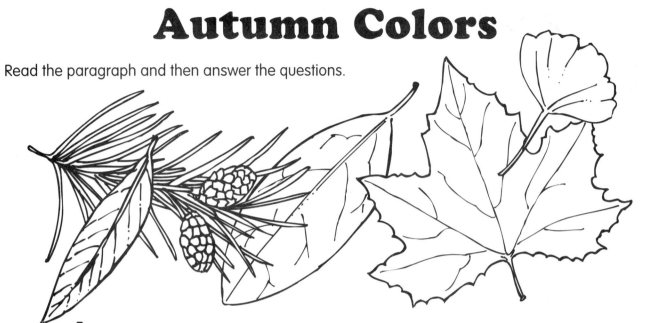

Autumn is a time of change in many types of trees. They shed their green leaves. They put on a bright coat of fall leaves. How does this change happen?

During the spring and summer, leaves produce food for the tree. The part of the leaf that is used in this process contains chlorophyll. Chlorophyll gives the leaves their green color. Leaves also contain orange and yellow. These colors are hidden by the green.

As days grow shorter and colder, changes occur in the leaves. A thin layer of cells grows over the water tubes in the leaves. Now no water can get into the leaf. The leaves stop making food. The chlorophyll breaks down and the green color disappears. This allows the yellow and orange colors to be seen. Finally, the leaves die and fall from the tree.

Not all trees have leaves that change color. Evergreen trees such as pines, cedars, and firs stay green all year round. Their tough, needlelike leaves can survive winter's cold.

1. What gives leaves their green color? What is its job? _____

   _____

2. What happens when the leaves can't get water? _____

   _____

3. How do you think evergreens got their name? _____

   _____

Autumn Word Search

Find the autumn words hidden in the word search. You will find words across, down, and diagonally.

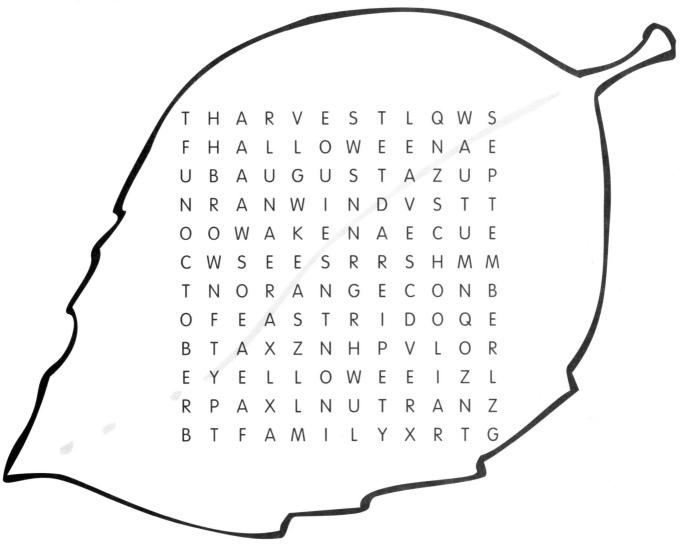

```
T  H  A  R  V  E  S  T  L  Q  W  S
F  H  A  L  L  O  W  E  E  N  A  E
U  B  A  U  G  U  S  T  A  Z  U  P
N  R  A  N  W  I  N  D  V  S  T  T
O  O  W  A  K  E  N  A  E  C  U  E
C  W  S  E  E  S  R  R  S  H  M  M
T  N  O  R  A  N  G  E  C  O  N  B
O  F  E  A  S  T  R  I  D  O  Q  E
B  T  A  X  Z  N  H  P  V  L  O  R
E  Y  E  L  L  O  W  E  E  I  Z  L
R  P  A  X  L  N  U  T  R  A  N  Z
B  T  F  A  M  I  L  Y  X  R  T  G
```

— Word Box —

August	family	harvest	orange	Thanksgiving
autumn	feast	leaves	red	weather
brown	fun	nut	school	wind
cool	Halloween	October	September	yellow
fall				

Name _____

Autumn Cinquain

Follow these steps to write a cinquain about autumn.

One word _____
(autumn topic)

Two words _____
(describe)

Three words _____
(an action)

Four Words _____
(a feeling)

One word _____
(repeat the topic or refer back to it)

Name _____

 # School Days

Circle each word as you find it. You will find words across, down, and diagonally.

```
E D U C A T I O N S C H O O L Z
B R T A T T E N D P A P E R U C
T U L I B R A R Y P F F U N N L
E M S X L E A R N Q E A G E C A
A P R I N C I P A L T N O Y H S
C D E C T E W S C I E N C E M S
H R P L A S R P M B R X T I X R
E A O U R S I E R R I Z U B L O
R W R E D S T L C O A C H A E O
O N T T Y U E L Q K M U S I C M
M A T H E M A T I C S G R A D E
R U N S T U D E N T O F F I C E
```

Word Box

art	grade	office	science
attend	gym	paper	spell
cafeteria	learn	pencil	student
classroom	library	principal	tardy
coach	lunch	recess	teacher
draw	mathematics	report	write
education	music	school	

List the words that name people at school.

_____   _____

_____   _____

Get Acquainted

Here is a chance for you to learn more about your new classmates. As you ask the questions, you can be making new friends.

Find a person that can answer "yes" to the question. Have the person sign his or her name on the line.

1. Do you have a baby sister? _____

2. Do you have a pet bird? _____

3. Have you ever flown on a plane? _____

4. Can you tap dance? _____

5. Can you speak a language other than English? _____

6. Do you know how to swim? _____

7. Did you go to camp last summer? _____

8. Do you have an autumn birthday? _____

9. Do you have hazel eyes? _____

10. Can you ride a horse? _____

11. Can you whistle? _____

12. Are you left-handed? _____

13. Have you ever tasted sushi? _____

14. Were you born in Texas? _____

 Seasonal Activities • EMC 2004 • © Evan-Moor Corp.

Back-to-School Crossword Puzzle

Use the clues to complete the crossword puzzle.

Across

1. a mealtime
4. a break between classes
7. the head person of the school
10. not at school on a school day
11. a tool for writing
12. lessons you do at home

Down

2. a place to eat lunch at school
3. a worktable at school
5. an instructor
6. a place to check out books
8. to look up information
9. to record words in some way

Name _____

Categories

Write the words in sets of things that go together.
Give each set a title that explains how the items are alike.

_____ title of set	_____ title of set
1. _____	1. _____
2. _____	2. _____
3. _____	3. _____
4. _____	4. _____
5. _____	5. _____
_____ title of set	_____ title of set
1. _____	1. _____
2. _____	2. _____
3. _____	3. _____
4. _____	4. _____
5. _____	5. _____

Word Box

books	gym	music	principal
cafeteria	history	office	reading
classroom	librarian	paint	science
coach	library	paper	student
computer	math	pencil	teacher

Seasonal Activities • EMC 2004 • © Evan-Moor Corp.

Around School

Draw a line to show George's path to the school bus.

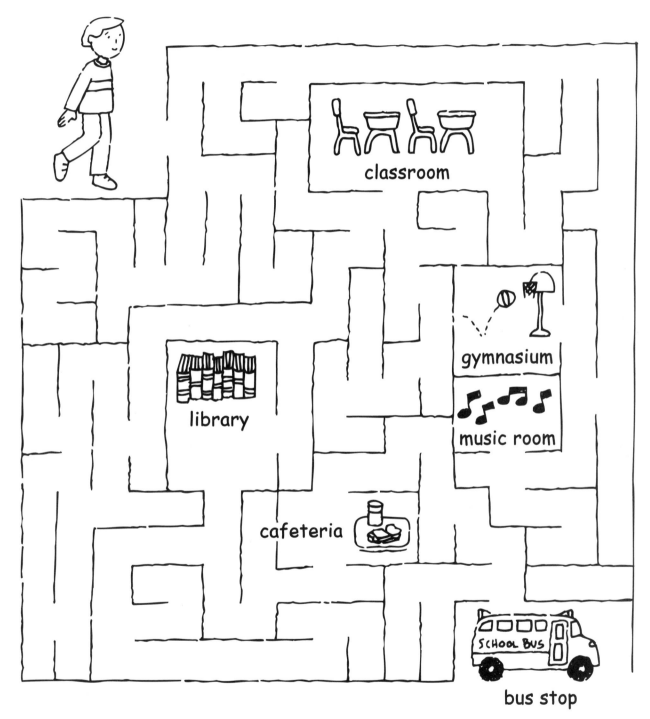

classroom

gymnasium

music room

library

cafeteria

SCHOOL BUS

bus stop

List in order the places he went on the way to the bus.

_____   _____   _____

Name _____

Native American Day

Read the paragraph and then answer the questions.

By the time the first explorers and settlers arrived from Europe, Native Americans had lived throughout North America for thousands of years. There were at least 600 tribes of Native Americans in North America. Each tribe had its own heritage, customs, and values.

Native Americans are not just a part of the past. Two and a half million Native Americans representing 500 tribes still live in the United States and Canada. They live and work in cities, rural areas, and on reservations. As well as being a part of modern society, Native Americans take pride in reviving tribal traditions and customs.

Many states have set aside a day to honor and celebrate Native Americans and their cultures.

1. Who were the first Americans?

_____

2. How were Native American tribes different from one another?

_____

3. Where do Native Americans live today?

_____

4. What does Native American Day celebrate?

_____

                        Seasonal Activities • EMC 2004 • © Evan-Moor Corp.

Name _____

About Native Americans

Read and then answer the questions.

- In 1492, Christopher Columbus arrived and thought that he was in India. He called all of the tribes "Indians" even though these people were scattered all over the continent, spoke different languages, and had different customs.

- There were over 300 Native American nations, speaking 143 different languages and 1,000 dialects, living in North America when the colonists arrived.

- The Native Americans traded deerskin and beaver pelts for metal products and cloth made by the colonists. European explorers, fur traders, and colonists of the 1600s learned how to make white birch bark canoes from the Native Americans in the Northeast.

- The Iroquois League of Nations formed the powerful, united Great Council. Benjamin Franklin observed a council meeting to learn about their form of government.

- By the late 1800s, most Native Americans had been forced by the U.S. government to live on reservations. Many Native Americans still live on these reservations. They proudly hold onto their tribal customs and teach the history of their people to their children. Other Native Americans live in cities and towns across the United States.

- In 1924, all Native Americans in the United States were made citizens.

1. Why did Columbus call the Native Americans "Indians"?

_____

_____

2. Are all Native American tribes alike? Explain your answer.

_____

_____

Name —————————————————————————

Native American Words

Early explorers and settlers borrowed many words from friendly Native Americans. Hundreds of these words are still being used today.

Find the hidden Native American words in the word search below.

```
T  S  U  C  C  O  T  A  S  H  X  M  S
O  C  H  I  P  M  U  N  K  R  R  U  Q
B  A  A  P  L  A  Y  M  P  Z  A  S  U
O  U  G  R  T  A  P  O  N  E  C  K  A
G  C  O  H  I  C  K  O  R  Y  C  R  S
G  U  N  O  P  B  A  S  E  N  O  A  H
A  S  E  T  I  L  O  E  K  X  O  T  N
N  O  P  P  O  S  S  U  M  U  N  U  T
S  M  O  C  C  A  S  I  N  R  N  Y  Z
T  O  M  A  H  A  W  K  A  Y  A  K  N
```

Word Box

caribou	moose	squash
caucus	muskrat	succotash
chipmunk	opossum	tipi
hickory	pecan	toboggan
kayak	raccoon	tomahawk
moccasin	skunk	

Seasonal Activities • EMC 2004 • © Evan-Moor Corp.

Columbus Day

Read the paragraph and then answer the questions.

October 12 is the day Christopher Columbus landed in the Western Hemisphere in 1492. He had set sail from Spain with three ships: the *Nina*, the *Pinta*, and the *Santa Maria*. About two months later, his ships reached land. Columbus thought he had reached the East Indies. Instead, he had reached the continent of North America. Columbus made four voyages to America. He never knew he had actually found lands that Europeans hadn't known about.

In 1937, President Roosevelt named October 12 a national holiday celebrating Columbus and his discovery.

Do you think Columbus's voyage was a success? Why or why not?

_____

_____

_____

Across the Atlantic

Study the map of Columbus's voyages across the Atlantic Ocean and then answer the questions.

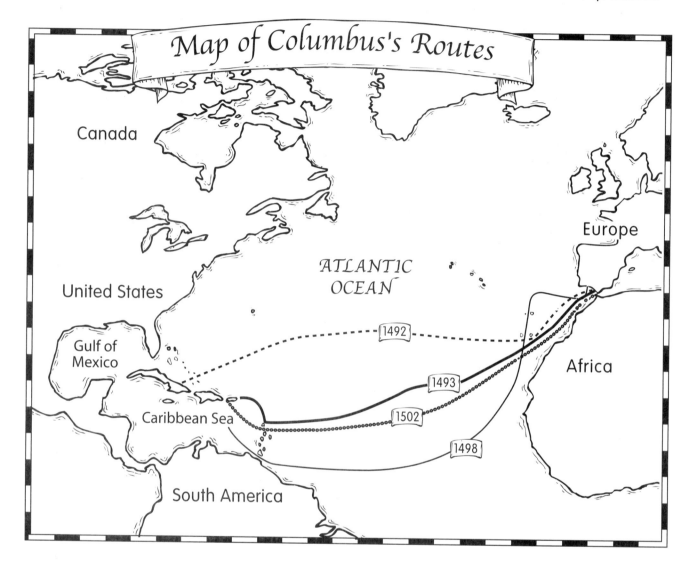

1. How many voyages did Christopher Columbus make to America? _____

2. In what year did he make his first voyage? his last voyage?

   _____   _____

3. Did Columbus ever land on the country we now call the United States?

   _____

   _____

All Aboard!

Draw what is in each box in the correct space on the grid. Use the numbers and letters to help you locate the space.

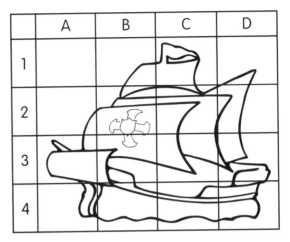

	A	B	C	D
1				
2				
3				
4				

Christopher Columbus's expedition included officers, sailors, a translator, three physicians, servants for each captain, a secretary, and an accountant. The main meal aboard ship was a stew of salted meat or fish, hard biscuits, and watered wine. The sailors slept on deck in good weather or found a spot below deck during storms.

Name _____

About Halloween

Read the paragraph and answer the question. Then draw yourself in the picture.

"**Trick or Treat!**" Halloween is a fun holiday for children in many parts of the world. Boys and girls of all ages wear masks and costumes and go from house to house shouting, "Trick or Treat!"

What do you like to do on Halloween? _____

_____

_____

_____

Seasonal Activities • EMC 2004 • © Evan-Moor Corp.

Name _____

Take a Close Look

Find 10 differences between the two pictures.

1 _____   6 _____

2 _____   7 _____

3 _____   8 _____

4 _____   9 _____

5 _____   10 _____

Name _____

Halloween Word Search

Circle the words in the word search.

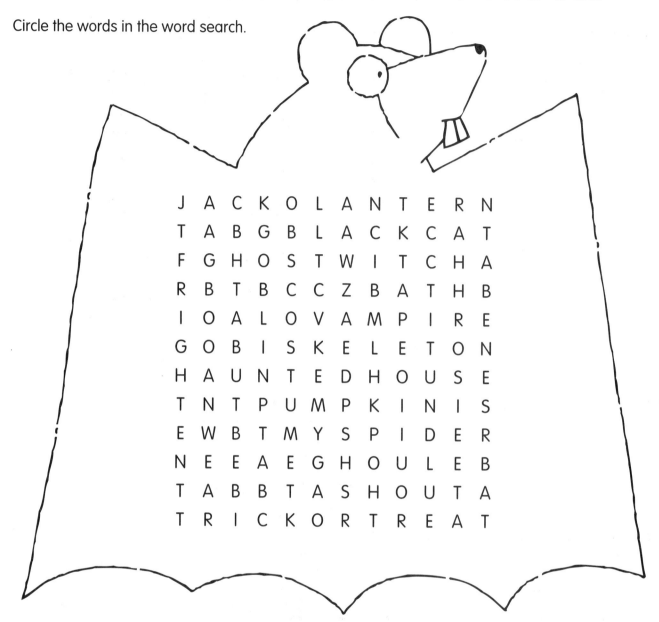

```
J A C K O L A N T E R N
T A B G B L A C K C A T
F G H O S T W I T C H A
R B T B C C Z B A T H B
I O A L O V A M P I R E
G O B I S K E L E T O N
H A U N T E D H O U S E
T N T P U M P K I N I S
E W B T M Y S P I D E R
N E E A E G H O U L E B
T A B B T A S H O U T A
T R I C K O R T R E A T
```

Word Box

bat	frighten	haunted house	skeleton	web
black cat	ghost	jack-o'-lantern	spider	witch
boo	ghoul	pumpkin	trick or treat	
costume	goblin	shout	vampire	

How many times can you find **BAT?** _____

(Hint: Some are backwards.)

Seasonal Activities • EMC 2004 • © Evan-Moor Corp.

Riddle Fun

Use the code to find the answers to the riddles.

A	L	G	⊏	N	O	U	⊡
B	⌐	H	⊐	O	⊡	V	⊟
C	⌐	I	⊐	P	⊔	W	⊡
D	⌐	J	C	Q	⌐	X	⊂
E	⊔	K	∪	R	⌐	Y	⊃
F	⊓	L	∪	S	⊔	Z	⊙
		M	∪	T	⊡		

What do you get if you cross a snowman and a vampire?

What kind of mistakes do ghosts make?

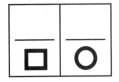

When a witch lands, where does she park?

Name _____

Jack-o'-lantern

How many words can you make using the letters in **jack-o'-lantern**?

_____ _____ _____
_____ _____ _____
_____ _____ _____
_____ _____ _____
_____ _____ _____
_____ _____ _____
_____ _____ _____
_____ _____ _____
_____ _____ _____

I made _____ words.

My longest word is _____.

My shortest word is _____.

Seasonal Activities • EMC 2004 • © Evan-Moor Corp.

Name _____

Halloween Surprise

Plot the pairs of numbers on the graph in the order they are listed. Count across and then up. Connect the points with straight lines. Start each new set of points with a new line. The first two have been done for you.

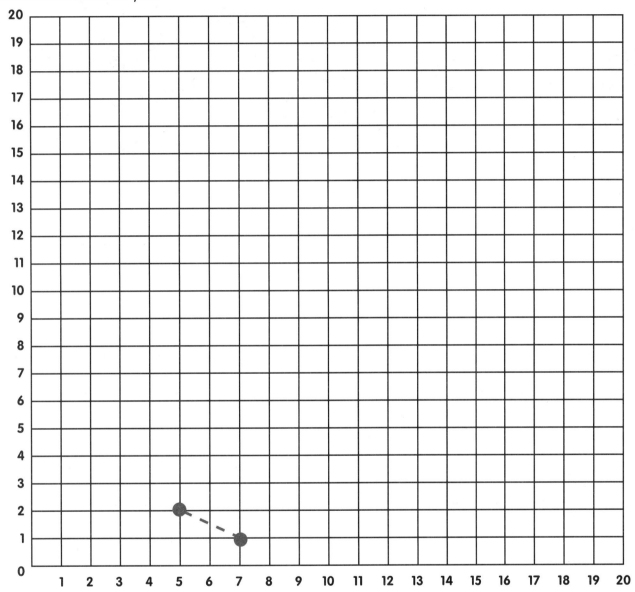

• (7,1) (5,2) (4,3) (3,4) (2,6) (2,8) (2,10) (3,12) (5,14) (7,15) (8,15) (10,15) (13,15) (15,14) (17,12) (18,10) (18,8) (18,6) (17,4) (16,3) (15,2) (13,1) (7,1) line ends

• (8,15) (7,18) (13,18) (12,15) line ends

• (5,9) (7,12) (9,9) (5,9) line ends

• (11,9) (13,12) (15,9) (11,9) line ends

• (9,7) (10,9) (11,7) (9,7) line ends

• (7,3) (6,5) (8,5) (8,4) (9,4) (9,5) (11,5) (11,4) (12,4) (12,5) (14,5) (13,3) (7,3) line ends

Name ———————————————

Trick or Treat!

Use the data on the chart to construct a bar graph on the blank graph. Then answer the questions.

Treats Alex Collected on Halloween

chocolate	gumdrops	jelly beans	pretzels	popcorn	sourballs
12	6	7	4	2	7

12						
10						
8						
6						
4						
2						
0	chocolate	gumdrops	jelly beans	pretzels	popcorn	sourballs

1. What is the total amount of treats collected by Alex? ————————————

2. What is your favorite Halloween treat? Why? ————————————

————————————————————————

————————————————————————

————————————————————————

————————————————————————

Seasonal Activities • EMC 2004 • © Evan-Moor Corp.

Name _____

Thanksgiving Day

Read the paragraph and then answer the questions.

Days of thanksgiving are celebrated all over the world. It is a day to give thanks for the blessings of the year.

In 1621, the Pilgrims had a feast to celebrate their first harvest in the New World. The feast lasted for three days. Governor Bradford of Plymouth Colony ordered this time for feasting and giving thanks.

The Thanksgiving Day we know became a national holiday in 1789. It is still a time to give thanks for our blessings. It is a time to celebrate with our friends and family.

1. What did the Pilgrims have to be thankful for in 1621?

_____

2. When was Thanksgiving made a national holiday?

_____

Name _____

Voyage to the New World

Read about the voyage of the *Mayflower.* Then answer the questions.

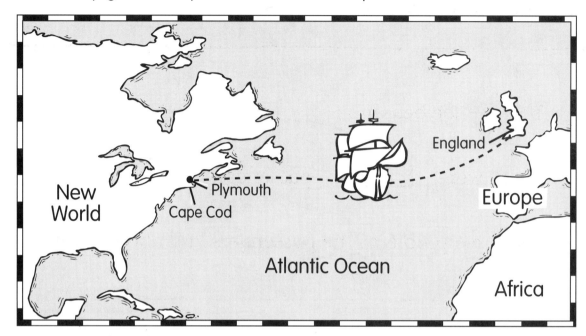

On September 6, 1620, a group of Pilgrims and other passengers left England. They set sail on a ship called the *Mayflower.* They sailed across the Atlantic Ocean to the New World.

There were 102 passengers and 30 crew members on the *Mayflower.* The captain's name was Christopher Jones. He worried about the journey. Was the ship too crowded? Were there enough supplies to last the entire journey? Would there be stormy seas?

Life was hard on the *Mayflower.* There was no privacy. There were no bathrooms. After a while, there was only dried meat and fish, dried fruit, cheese, and hard biscuits to eat. The Pilgrims kept their spirits up by praying, singing, and telling stories.

On November 11, after 66 days, the ship reached land. The *Mayflower* landed in a safe harbor at the tip of Cape Cod. The Pilgrims had made it to the New World.

Would you have made the journey to the New World? Why or why not?

_____

_____

_____

Seasonal Activities • EMC 2004 • © Evan-Moor Corp.

Note: Use this page after students have read the material on page 28.

The *Mayflower* Voyage

Fill in the blanks to complete the page.

The voyage began on _____.

There were _____ passengers.

List three problems the passengers had aboard ship.

1. _____

2. _____

3. _____

They landed at the tip of _____.

The voyage lasted _____ days.

They reached land on _____.

Name _____

The Mayflower

Count by 2s to connect the dots.

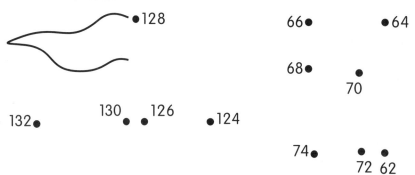

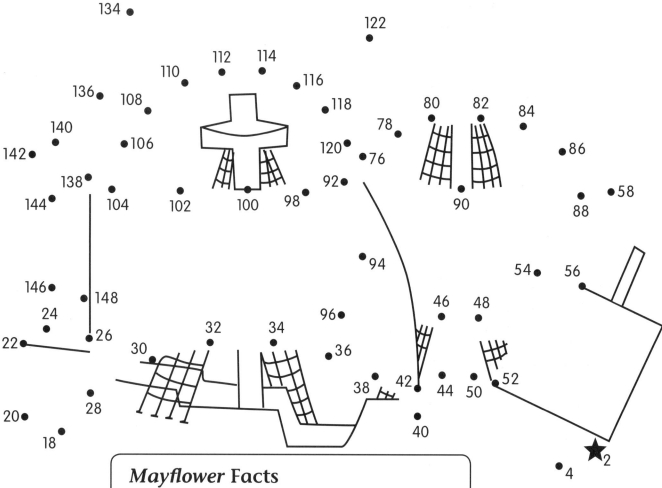

Mayflower Facts

- The ship was 90 feet (27 meters) long.
- It weighed 180 tons (162 metric tonnes).
- It carried 102 passengers.

Seasonal Activities • EMC 2004 • © Evan-Moor Corp.

The First Year

Read about the Pilgrims and then answer the questions.

The Pilgrims chose land near a small bay as a place to live. They called their settlement Plymouth. They lived on board the ship until they could build homes. When weather permitted, many of the settlers went ashore and cut down timber to build temporary shelters.

In March, the weather improved. The settlers were able to start work on family gardens. They were able to build permanent houses. They planted seeds from England. These seeds did not grow well in the rocky soil. These early Pilgrims did not know how to hunt or fish, so food was running low. The arrival of two Native Americans brought the help the settlers needed.

Squanto, a Patuxet Indian, taught them how to hunt. He showed them how to plant native plants. Samoset, an Abnaki Indian, and Squanto reassured the local Wampanoag Indians that the Pilgrims were peaceful. The Pilgrims were thankful to the Indians for helping them survive their first year in the New World.

1. What problems did the settlers face?

   _____

   _____

2. What type of help did Samoset and Squanto provide for the Pilgrims?

   _____

   _____

   _____

Name ———————————————

A Peace Treaty

Read about the treaty and then answer the questions.

In 1621, the Pilgrims of Plymouth Colony and the Wampanoag tribe agreed to a peace treaty that would last 50 years. The Pilgrims needed the Wampanoag to help them learn how to survive in this new land. The Wampanoag wanted to find an ally to help them fight their enemies, the Narraganset. Squanto helped negotiate this treaty between the Pilgrims and Chief Massasoit. It was the first known treaty of its kind.

1. Why did the Wampanoag tribe sign a peace treaty with the Pilgrims?

_____

2. Why did the Pilgrims need to sign a peace treaty with the Wampanoag tribe?

_____

3. Can you think of a reason why the treaty was broken after fifty years?

_____

_____

Seasonal Activities • EMC 2004 • © Evan-Moor Corp.

Name _____

Working in Plymouth Colony

While most people in Plymouth Colony were farmers, raising grains for cornmeal and flour, and raising cows, pigs, sheep, and chickens for food and wool, there were also craftspeople who made things for other people. For example, the farmer took his grain to the miller, who ground it into flour for the farmer.

- The **blacksmith** made things out of iron.
- The **cobbler** fixed shoes and boots.
- The **cooper** made wooden barrels.
- The **hatter** made plain and fancy hats.
- The **miller** ground the grains into flour.
- The **housewright** built houses.

Find the bolded words above as well as the words below in the word search.

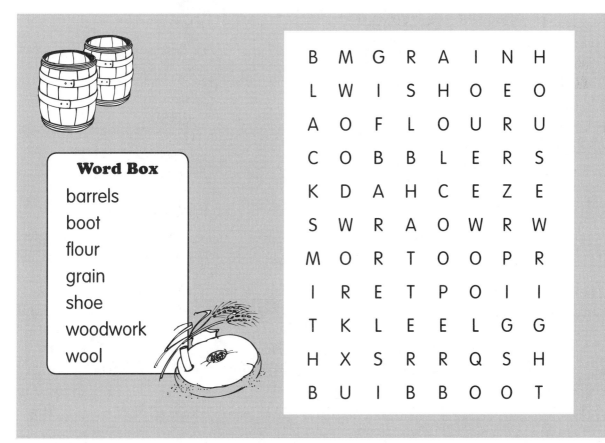

Word Box

barrels
boot
flour
grain
shoe
woodwork
wool

B	M	G	R	A	I	N	H
L	W	I	S	H	O	E	O
A	O	F	L	O	U	R	U
C	O	B	B	L	E	R	S
K	D	A	H	C	E	Z	E
S	W	R	A	O	W	R	W
M	O	R	T	O	O	P	R
I	R	E	T	P	O	I	I
T	K	L	E	E	L	G	G
H	X	S	R	R	Q	S	H
B	U	I	B	B	O	O	T

Making Butter

This Pilgrim girl is helping her mother by churning butter. Make both sides of the girl and butter churn the same to complete the picture.

Women and girls were in charge of the garden and farm animals. They spun wool to make cloth and sewed all the clothes and bedding for the family. They made their own soap and candles. They turned milk into butter and cheese. Mothers taught their daughters all of these skills.

Thanksgiving Crossword Puzzle

Use the clues below to solve the crossword puzzle.

Across

2. the Native American who taught the Pilgrims how to plant and hunt in the New World

5. the ship the Pilgrims traveled on

6. the colony founded by the Pilgrims

8. the number of years the peace treaty with the Wampanoags lasted

9. the country from which the Pilgrims set sail

Down

1. the Native Americans who were living in the area where the Pilgrims settled

3. the number of days the thanksgiving feast lasted

4. the ocean the Pilgrims crossed to get to the New World

7. gathering crops in the fall

Name _____

New World Food Plants

Circle the foods that came from the New World.

```
B C P O T A T O A R A S I N
L H H E S U C C O T A S H O
D I A G A J C O C O A Q M T
E L M G P N A C R R L U M E
C I R A W L U M X N P A A P
O P E N B A N T D L U S I O
F E X C I E V M F E M H Z P
F P O S U G A R M A P L E C
E P B E E P Y N Z K K O N O
G E T O M A T O S T I R H R
A R Y H P I K C L E N B E N
```

Make a red check in the boxes in front of the foods you have tasted.

Word Box

- ☐ chili pepper
- ☐ cocoa
- ☐ corn
- ☐ lima beans
- ☐ maize
- ☐ peanut
- ☐ popcorn
- ☐ potato
- ☐ pumpkin
- ☐ squash
- ☐ sugar maple
- ☐ tomato

Seasonal Activities • EMC 2004 • © Evan-Moor Corp.

Thanksgiving Riddles

Multiply and then use the code to answer the riddles.

8 x 5 = ———— **a**   8 x 7 = ———— **m**

9 x 9 = ———— **c**   5 x 3 = ———— **n**

7 x 6 = ———— **d**   7 x 7 = ———— **o**

3 x 9 = ———— **e**   9 x 6 = ———— **p**

9 x 2 = ———— **f**   8 x 9 = ———— **r**

12 x 12 = ———— **g**   8 x 8 = ———— **s**

8 x 6 = ———— **h**   6 x 6 = ———— **t**

7 x 5 = ———— **i**   9 x 5 = ———— **u**

9 x 7 = ———— **k**   5 x 4 = ———— **v**

8 x 3 = ———— **l**   10 x 10 = ———— **y**

Why was the turkey the drummer of the band?

—— ——   —— —— ——   —— —— ——
48 27   48 40 42   36 48 27

—— —— —— —— —— —— —— —— —— ——
42 72 45 56 64 36 35 81 63 64

What do you get if you cross a turkey with a centipede?

—— —— —— —— —— —— —— —— —— ——
42 72 45 56 64 36 35 81 63 64

—— —— ——   —— —— —— —— —— —— —— —— ——
16 49 72   27 20 27 72 100 49 15 27

Name _____

A Feast of Thanksgiving

Read the story and then answer the questions.

A feast of thanksgiving was held in October 1621. This three-day harvest celebration included 52 English colonists and 91 Wampanoag Indians. The colonists were grateful to the Indians for helping them survive the first year. In English style, Chief Massasoit and his leaders ate with the leading men of the colony at a "high table," which probably featured the best foods. Tables were set up both indoors and outdoors for the other guests.

The colonists invited the Wampanoag Indians to their feast.

Who would you invite to your Thanksgiving feast? Why?_____

_____

_____

_____

   Seasonal Activities • EMC 2004 • © Evan-Moor Corp.

Name —————————————————

I Am Thankful

List the things that you are thankful for this autumn.

In the autumn of 1621, the Pilgrims gave thanks for their bountiful harvest.

Things I Am Thankful For

1. _____

2. _____

3. _____

4. _____

5. _____

6. _____

7. _____

8. _____

9. _____

10. _____

Name _____

Let's Eat!

Unscramble the words to find what foods were served at the first thanksgiving feast.

kinpumsp _____   soeog _____

nipturs _____   macls _____

nroc _____   soyters _____

ered _____   bagcabe _____

keytur _____   lee _____

cudk _____   soblter _____

Word Box

cabbage	deer	goose	pumpkins
clams	duck	lobster	turkey
corn	eel	oysters	turnips

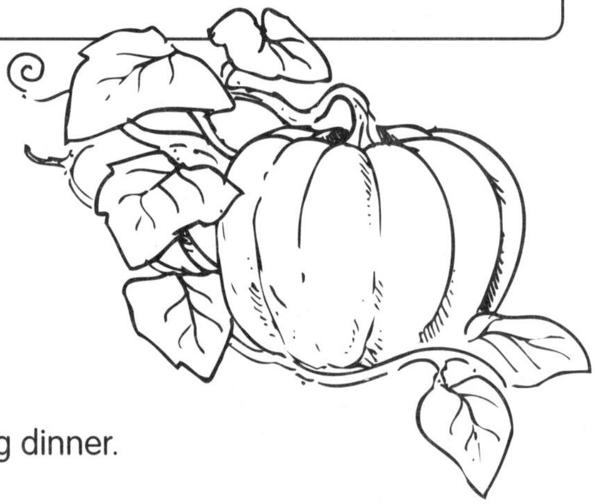

Does your family celebrate Thanksgiving?
If you answered "yes," list what you eat for Thanksgiving dinner.

_____   _____

_____   _____

_____   _____

_____   _____

Seasonal Activities • EMC 2004 • © Evan-Moor Corp.

Winter

December Holidays

Winter Holidays

Presidents

Name It

Write a word beginning with a letter in **winter** under each category.

	an animal	something to eat	a country	something to wear	a girl's name
Example A	anteater	artichoke	Australia	anklets	Anna
W					
I					
N					
T					
E					
R					

Seasonal Activities • EMC 2004 • © Evan-Moor Corp.

Name _____

Snow Words

Write the word for each definition. All answers contain the word **snow**.
Then write the circled letters in order on these lines:

___ ___ ___ ___ ___ ___ ___
1   2   3   4   5   6   7

1. small white flakes falling from the sky

2. a small round mass of snow packed together

3. a warm garment worn by children in very cold weather

4. a device used to push or throw snow off a road

5. a motor vehicle used to travel over snow

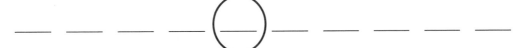

6. a heap of snow blown together by the wind

7. wooden and leather frames worn on feet when walking on snow

✏ Draw the mystery object on the back of this page.

Name _____

Winter Word Search

Find these winter words and circle them.

Word Box

blizzard
chilly
coat
cold
earmuffs
freeze
frost
gloves
goosebumps
hat
icicle
scarf
sled
snow
wet
wind

```
S  L  E  D  F  R  O  S  T  W
C  N  E  A  R  M  U  F  F  S
G  O  O  S  E  B  U  M  P  S
L  T  L  W  E  W  I  N  D  C
O  A  N  D  Z  C  O  A  T  A
V  H  T  T  E  N  S  W  E  R
E  I  C  I  C  L  E  P  W  F
S  B  L  I  Z  Z  A  R  D  T
V  F  U  N  C  H  I  L  L  Y
```

Does it snow in the winter where you live?

yes   no

Seasonal Activities • EMC 2004 • © Evan-Moor Corp.

Name _____

Winter Haiku

Write a haiku about winter.

A **haiku** has 3 lines and 17 syllables.

It usually refers to the seasons or something in nature.

Line 1—5 syllables

Line 2—7 syllables

Line 3—5 syllables

Start with the thought and then adjust the syllables.

_____

five syllables

_____

seven syllables

_____

five syllables

What's for Breakfast?

Count by 12s and then use the code to answer the riddle.

A _____   K _____   R _____

D _____   L _____   S _____

E _____   O _____   T _____

F _____

What do snowmen eat for breakfast?

___ ___ ___ ___ ___ ___ ___
48   96   84   108   120   36   24

___ ___ ___ ___ ___ ___
48   72   12   60   36   108

What do you like to eat for breakfast on a cold day?

_____

_____

_____

_____

_____

          Seasonal Activities • EMC 2004 • © Evan-Moor Corp.

Bill of Rights Day

Read about the Bill of Rights and then answer the questions.

December 15 is "Bill of Rights Day." It celebrates the first ten additions, called amendments, to the Constitution of the United States. These ten amendments were added to protect freedoms such as freedom of religion, freedom of speech, and freedom of the press.

More than 11,000 possible amendments have been introduced in Congress. The original ten in the Bill of Rights became law on December 15, 1791. Since that time, only seventeen more have received enough votes to be added to the Constitution.

1. How many amendments to the Constitution are there now?

   _____

2. Our Constitution gives us many freedoms. As good citizens, we also have responsibilities. What can you do to be a good citizen?

   _____

   _____

   _____

   _____

Name —————————————————————

 # A Recipe for a Winter Holiday

Circle the holiday you are going to write about.

Christmas   Hanukkah   Kwanzaa

1. Think about what "ingredients" make the holiday special for your family.

   people   activities   food

   places   decorations   memories

   ———————————————   ———————————————   ———————————————

2. Now write your "recipe."

My Recipe for a Perfect ———————————————————————————

Ingredients:———————————————   ———————————————

———————————————   ———————————————

———————————————   ———————————————

Directions: ——————————————————————————————————

——

——

——

——

——

——

Name _____

Christmas

Read about Christmas and then answer the questions.

Christmas is a celebration of the birth of Jesus. On December 25, Christians around the world celebrate His birth with church services, the giving of gifts, the singing of carols, and family gatherings.

1. Who celebrates Christmas?

_____

2. How is the holiday celebrated?

_____

3. Does your family celebrate Christmas? _____

   If yes, how do you celebrate? _____

_____

The Christmas Story Word Search

Circle the Christmas words hidden in the word search.

```
L O S J E S U S X D
S J P T Z R O W N O
H A O L A P X I A N
E M N S A R E S T K
P A I G E M N E I E
H R V N E P B M V Y
E Y E R N L H E I B
R S T A B L E N T A
D X M A N G E R Y B
B E T H L E H E M Y
```

Word Box

angel	inn	manger	shepherd
baby	Jesus	Mary	stable
Bethlehem	Joseph	nativity	star
donkey	lamb	oxen	Wise Men

Seasonal Activities • EMC 2004 • © Evan-Moor Corp.

Name _____

We Three Kings

Help the Three Kings
reach Bethlehem.

The Three Kings brought gifts to the baby Jesus.
What gift would you take to the new baby?

_____

_____

Las Posadas

Count by 3s to connect the dots.
Read the story and then answer
the questions.

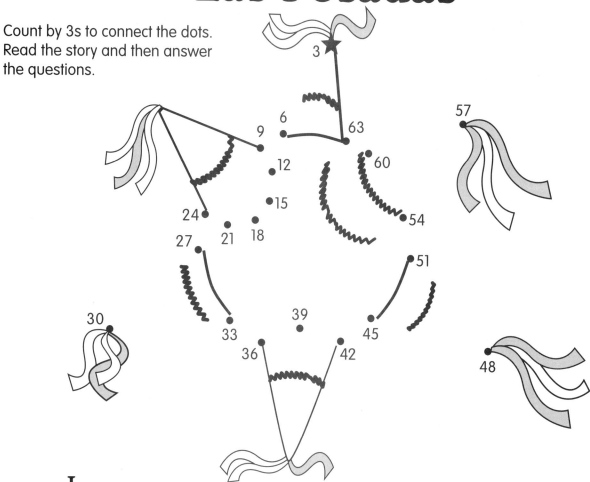

In Mexico, beginning on December 16 and continuing for the next nine nights, Posadas processions reenact Mary and Joseph's search for lodging in Bethlehem. A parade of children carrying lanterns and platforms with figures of Mary and Joseph stop at homes of neighbors and beg to be taken in. When they reach a prearranged house, the manger is carried in, prayers are said, and refreshments are served. A piñata is often the highlight of the party.

1. How long does the celebration last? _____

2. What is the purpose of Las Posadas? _____

_____

3. Does your family celebrate this holiday? _____

If yes, how do you celebrate? _____

_____

Name _____

Merry Christmas Crossword Puzzle

Use the clues to solve the crossword puzzle.

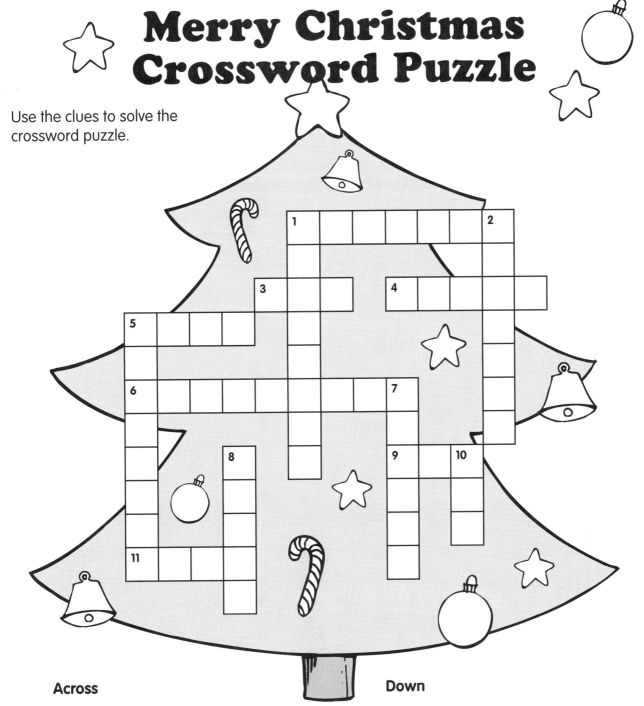

Across

1. a reindeer with a shiny red nose
3. an evergreen tree
4. a plant with prickly leaves and red berries
5. white lacy flakes that fall from the sky
6. decorations for a Christmas tree
9. the night before a holiday
11. another name for "present"

Down

1. eight of these pull Santa's sleigh
2. a special day for celebration
5. some children hang this above the fireplace on Christmas Eve
7. a vehicle for traveling over snow
8. a chubby man who is supposed to bring presents to good children
10. a worker in Santa's workshop

Name _____

Take a Close Look

Find 10 differences between the two pictures.

1. _____

_____

2. _____

_____

3. _____

_____

4. _____

_____

5. _____

_____

6. _____

_____

7. _____

_____

8. _____

_____

9. _____

_____

10. _____

_____

Name That Christmas Tune!

Use the code to name some favorite old Christmas songs.

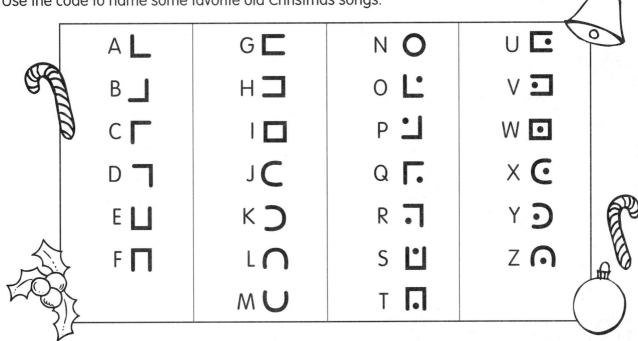

1.

2.

3.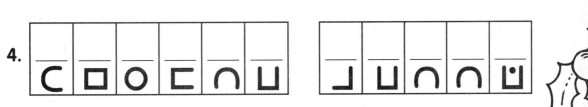

4.

Write the name of your favorite Christmas song in code.

————————————————————————————————

Name _____

Celebrate Hanukkah

Read about Hanukkah and then answer the questions.

People celebrate Hanukkah to remember a miracle. Judah the Maccabee fought the Syrians for three years. When he and his men finally defeated the Syrians, they reclaimed their temple. The temple was cleaned and the Jewish soldiers relit the Lamp of Eternal Light. They had only enough oil for one day, and it would take eight days to get more oil. Incredibly, the oil lasted for eight days.

Hanukkah begins on the twenty-fifth day of the Jewish month of Kislev and lasts for eight days. During Hanukkah, families gather every night to light the menorah. Traditional foods served during the celebration include potato pancakes, called latkes, and applesauce. Children receive small gifts on each of the eight nights and play with a square-sided top called a dreidel.

1. How is Hanukkah celebrated? _____

_____

2. Does your family celebrate Hanukkah? _____

If yes, how do you celebrate? _____

_____

Seasonal Activities • EMC 2004 • © Evan-Moor Corp.

Name _____

The Dreidel Game

Read about the dreidel game and then answer the question.

A dreidel is a four-sided top. Each side has a single Hebrew letter. The letters have a double meaning. They stand for a phrase that means "A great miracle happened there." They also stand for Yiddish words that give rules for the dreidel game.

How to Play:

- Give each player the same number of tokens (any small item such as raisins).
- Each player puts one token in the pot.
- The first player spins the dreidel and reads the symbol that lands faceup. The symbols tell the player what to do.

    hey = half (take 1/2 of the tokens in the pot)

    gimel = everything (take all the tokens in the pot)

    nun = nothing (take nothing from the pot)

    shin = put in (put in another token)

- Each player takes a turn.
- When the cup is empty, each player puts in another token.

Four people are playing. They each put 1 token in the pot. After each spin, how many tokens remain in the pot?

ה Spin 1: hey	נ Spin 2: nun	ג Spin 3: gimel	ש Spin 4: shin
_____	_____	_____	_____

Name _____

About Kwanzaa

Read about Kwanzaa and then answer the questions.

This African-American holiday was established in 1966. Kwanzaa means "first fruits" in Swahili. The holiday is based on festivals in Africa that celebrate the gathering of crops that feed the community. In the U.S., African Americans celebrate their history and culture and honor their ancestors during the holiday. Homes are decorated. People gather to eat good food and to share music, dancing, and traditional storytelling.

On each of the seven days of Kwanzaa, a candle is lit for one of the seven basic values of African-American family life. The seven values are unity, self-determination, collective work and responsibility, cooperative economics, purpose, creativity, and faith.

1. Who celebrates Kwanzaa?

   _____

2. Why is it celebrated?

   _____

3. Does your family celebrate Kwanzaa? _____

   If yes, how do you celebrate? _____

   _____

　　　　Seasonal Activities • EMC 2004 • © Evan-Moor Corp.

Light the Kinara

Follow the steps at the bottom of the page to color the candles.

On each of the seven days of Kwanzaa, a candle is lit. Each candle represents one of the seven basic values of African-American life.

Day 1 Color the middle candle black.
This candle stands for **unity**.

Day 2 Color the candle to the left of the middle candle red.
This candle stands for **self-determination**.

Day 3 Color the candle to the right of the middle candle green.
This candle stands for **collective work and responsibility**.

Day 4 Color the candle to the left of the red candle red.
This candle stands for **cooperative economics**.

Day 5 Color the candle to the right of the green candle green.
This candle stands for **purpose**.

Day 6 Color the last candle on the left red.
This candle stands for **creativity**.

Day 7 Color the last candle on the right green.
This candle stands for **faith**.

Name _____

Happy 20___ ___!

Read about New Year's and answer the questions. Then draw yourself in the celebration.

New Year's Day celebrations mark the end of an old year and the start of a new year. All over the world, the new year is greeted with noise. The custom of a noisy greeting at midnight goes back to an ancient belief that noise will scare away evil spirits. This makes room for the good spirits to come and bless the new year.

While we celebrate the new year on January 1 in the United States, cultures using different calendars celebrate at other times of the year.

1. What are loud noises on New Year's Eve supposed to do?

_____

2. On what date do we celebrate the new year in the U.S.?

_____

3. Do you stay up until midnight on New Year's Eve? _____

_____

Seasonal Activities • EMC 2004 • © Evan-Moor Corp.

The Months of the Year

Unscramble the names of the months of the year. Then write the months in the order in which they occur in the year.

Unscrambled Months	Months in Order

aym   _____ May _____   1. _____

bruryafe   _____   2. _____

guutsa   _____   3. _____

bemdecer   _____   4. _____

aanuryj   _____   5. _____ May _____

bemveron   _____   6. _____

neuj   _____   7. _____

bemtseerp   _____   8. _____

harmc   _____   9. _____

yulj   _____   10. _____

terbooc   _____   11. _____

ripla   _____   12. _____

Name _____

★ New Year's Resolutions

Many people use the first day of a new year to think about themselves. They think about habits they would like to break. They think about new things they would like to learn or do. Think about changes you would like to make. Think about what your resolutions might be.

Write a list of resolutions for the new year.

1. _____

2. _____

3. _____

4. _____

5. _____

6. _____

7. _____

8. _____

9. _____

10. _____

Seasonal Activities • EMC 2004 • © Evan-Moor Corp.

Dr. Martin Luther King, Jr.
A Modern Hero

Read about Dr. King and then answer the questions.

Martin Luther King, Jr., was a great American. He was a leader in the civil rights movement in the United States. He believed in using nonviolent means to bring about equality for all people. In 1963, there was a march for civil rights in Washington, D.C. Dr. King spoke about his dream that the United States would be true to the idea that all people are equal. He received the Nobel Peace Prize for his work.

He was assassinated on April 4, 1968. The third Monday in January is celebrated as a national holiday to honor Dr. King. This is a day for all Americans to think about how to reach the goal of equal rights for everyone.

1. In what important movement did Martin Luther King, Jr., take part?

_____

_____

2. What was his dream for the people of the United States?

_____

_____

3. Why do you think he won the Nobel Peace Prize?

_____

_____

Name —————————————————————

Martin Luther King, Jr.
Crossword Puzzle

Use the clues to complete the crossword puzzle.

Word Box

boycott	justice	protest
civil rights	march	segregation
discrimination	nonviolence	speech
dream	peace	struggle

Seasonal Activities • EMC 2004 • © Evan-Moor Corp.

Across

1. to work hard to solve a difficult problem or situation

3. a strongly held purpose or goal

5. freedom from violence, war, or hostility

6. to walk together as a group

9. refusing to use violent means to achieve a goal

10. an action by a person or group seeking change

11. fairness according to principles of right and wrong

Down

1. a public address

2. treating others in an unfair way because of race, religion, etc.

4. the practice of separating a group from the rest of society

7. certain privileges guaranteed to everyone by law

8. to act with others to stop buying or using things

Name —————————————————

Groundhog Day

Complete the picture. Then read about Groundhog Day and answer the question.

On February 2, tradition says that groundhogs come out of their holes in the ground and tell the world whether there will be an early or a late spring. If the groundhog comes out of his burrow and sees his shadow, he will run back into his burrow and winter will last another six weeks. However, if the day is cloudy, the groundhog will not see his shadow and will stay outside and there will be an early spring.

Is this story a myth or not? Explain your answer. ————————————

————————————————————————————————

————————————————————————————————

————————————————————————————————

   Seasonal Activities • EMC 2004 • © Evan-Moor Corp.

Name _____

Who Am I?

Use division to help you find my name.

Some people say I forecast the weather. Look out if I see my shadow!

A - 2	
E - 3	
H - 4	
I - 5	
L - 6	
N - 7	
P - 8	
S - 9	
T - 10	
U - 11	
W - 12	
X - 13	
Y - 14	

☐ $72 \div 9 =$ _____

☐ $99 \div 9 =$ _____

☐ $56 \div 8 =$ _____

☐ $182 \div 14 =$ _____

☐ $81 \div 9 =$ _____

☐ $275 \div 25 =$ _____

☐ $100 \div 10 =$ _____

☐ $100 \div 50 =$ _____

☐ $144 \div 12 =$ _____

☐ $140 \div 20 =$ _____

☐ $99 \div 33 =$ _____

☐ $42 \div 3 =$ _____

☐ $88 \div 11 =$ _____

☐ $36 \div 9 =$ _____

☐ $80 \div 16 =$ _____

☐ $72 \div 12 =$ _____

Color the picture that shows what kind of animal I am.

Weather Watch

Punxsutawney Phil is a nervous groundhog. What will happen when he peeks out of his burrow? Will he see his shadow? Will it be raining? What will the weather be? Find the words below that describe weather. Write them in the box.

afraid	bright	foggy	hazy	rainy	terrified
alarmed	brisk	foul	jumpy	shy	uneasy
angry	cautious	frightened	nervous	skittish	upset
balmy	cloudy	gusty	overcast	stormy	windy
breezy	excited	happy	pleasant	sunshiny	

What do the remaining words describe? _____

   Seasonal Activities • EMC 2004 • © Evan-Moor Corp.

Name _____

Chinese New Year

Read about Chinese New Year and
then answer the questions.
Count by 2s to connect the dots.

"**Gung Hay Fat Choy!**" Chinese New Year occurs on the first day
of the first new moon after January 21. To get ready for the new year,
families clean their houses from top to bottom. They wear new clothing.
Good luck wishes are hung from windows. Children receive little red
packets with coins inside.

The celebration includes a parade led by a long dragon, the symbol
of good luck. People hold up the dragon and make it dance and weave
through the streets. The dragon dance is believed to chase away bad
luck. Firecrackers explode as the dragon passes.

1. Why doesn't Chinese New Year occur on the same day every year?

_____

2. How would you greet someone on Chinese New Year?

_____

Name _____

Note: Reproduce page 71 to use with this page.

Tangrams

It is believed that the tangram puzzle originated in China about 250 years ago.

Use your tangram pieces to make this rooster in the box.

Seasonal Activities • EMC 2004 • © Evan-Moor Corp.

Note: Reproduce page 70 to use with this page.

Color these puzzle pieces. Then cut them apart and arrange to make the tangram rooster.

Name —————————————————————————

What Animal Are You?

In the Chinese calendar, each year is named for an animal. People born in the same year are thought to be like that animal. Your animal depends on the year you were born. Use the chart to find the name of the animal for that year. Fill in the blanks to complete the sentences.

I was born in _____. My animal is _____ .

My animal traits are _____ ,

and _____ .

	Animal	Year	Character Traits
	Rat	1984, 1996	friendly, creative, hardworking
	Ox	1985, 1997	strong, loyal, honest
	Tiger	1986, 1998	brave, earnest, hasty
	Rabbit	1987, 1999	shy, quiet, humble
	Dragon	1988, 2000	strong, imaginative, decisive
	Snake	1989, 2001	tricky, subtle, controlled
	Horse	1990, 2002	cheerful, talented, competitive
	Sheep	1991, 2003	trusting, artistic, obedient
	Monkey	1992, 2004	funny, inventive, mischievous
	Rooster	1993, 2005	proud, confident, determined
	Dog	1994, 2006	trustworthy, likeable, loyal
	Pig	1995, 2007	hardworking, caring, industrious

Do you think you are like the animal that represents the year you were born?

Why or why not? _____

_____

   Seasonal Activities • EMC 2004 • © Evan-Moor Corp.

Name _____

Presidents' Day

Read about Presidents' Day and then answer the questions.

The birthdays of Abraham Lincoln (February 12) and George Washington (February 22) were once celebrated as separate holidays. Since 1971, both presidents have been honored on the same day, the third Monday in February. Presidents' Day is a day to honor all of America's past presidents.

1. Before 1971, when were Lincoln's and Washington's birthdays celebrated?

_____

2. Why do you think we celebrate Presidents' Day instead of Washington's

birthday and Lincoln's birthday? _____

_____

George Washington

Draw President Washington's face by following the grid.
Then read about Washington's life.

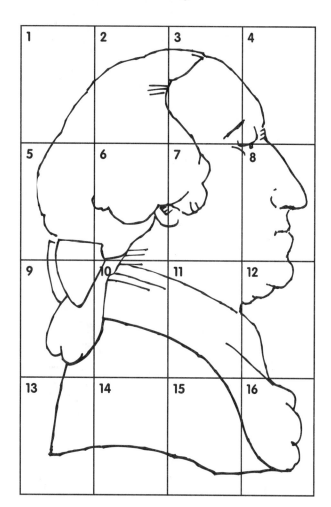

1	2	3	4
5	6	7	8
9	10	11	12
13	14	15	16

About George Washington, America's first president.

- Washington was born in Virginia on February 22, 1732.
- He was a surveyor, a soldier, and a farmer.
- He was commander-in-chief of the Army during the Revolutionary War.
- He was called the "father of our country."
- His wife was Martha Dandridge Washington.
- His family home was called Mount Vernon.
- He died of illness in 1799.

Seasonal Activities • EMC 2004 • © Evan-Moor Corp.

Name _____

Abraham Lincoln

Draw the other side of President Lincoln. Then read about Lincoln's life.

About Abraham Lincoln, the 16th president:

- Lincoln was born in a log cabin in Kentucky on February 12, 1809.
- He was a rail-splitter and a lawyer.
- He was called "honest Abe."
- His wife was Mary Todd Lincoln.
- He was president during the Civil War.
- He was assassinated in 1865.

Seasonal Activities • EMC 2004 • © Evan-Moor Corp.

Name _____

 # Two Presidents

Write the facts next to the correct president.

1. _____
2. _____
3. _____
4. _____
5. _____
6. _____
7. _____
8. _____

1. _____
2. _____
3. _____
4. _____
5. _____
6. _____
7. _____
8. _____

1st president of the U.S.
16th president of the U.S.
called "Honest Abe"
called the "father of our country"
was a farmer and surveyor
was a rail-splitter and lawyer
born in Virginia on Feb. 22, 1732
born in Kentucky on Feb. 12, 1809

family home called Mount Vernon
born in a log cabin
married Mary Todd
married Martha Dandridge
general in the Revolutionary War
president during the Civil War
shot and killed in 1865
died of illness in 1799

Seasonal Activities • EMC 2004 • © Evan-Moor Corp.

President Word Search

Circle the presidents' names in the word search.

```
K M E N W I L S O N E M A C L
H A C I A F T Y L E R C S L G
A D A M S M O N R O E K H E A
R I R B H E T R O P D I J V R
D S T U I E N A D R O N A E F
I O E S N N I H Y A T L C L I
N N R H G R E G O L L E K A E
G F F S T A F T R W O Y S N L
P I O N O L S O N A E R O D D
I L L I N C O L N S N R N I E
E L W X R E A G A N A T I N A
R M H O O V E R J O H N S O N
C O I N O A R T T R U M A N C
E R S U S N B U C H A N A N L
J E F F E R S O N A R T H U I
A L D O V A N B U R E N E A N
K E N N E D Y A R T H U R H T
E C O O L I D G E H A Y E S O
G I L L T H A R R I S O N S N
```

Word Box

Adams	Fillmore	Johnson	Reagan
Arthur	Ford	Kennedy	Roosevelt
Buchanan	Garfield	Lincoln	Taft
Bush	Grant	Madison	Taylor
Carter	Harding	McKinley	Truman
Cleveland	Harrison	Monroe	Tyler
Coolidge	Hayes	Nixon	Van Buren
Clinton	Hoover	Pierce	Washington
Coolidge	Jackson	Polk	Wilson
Eisenhower	Jefferson		

Name ——————————————————

Saint Valentine's Day

Color the three valentines that are the same.

About This Day

There was a priest in Rome around A.D. 270 named Saint Valentine. He probably didn't have anything to do with our Valentine's Day. In fact, no one is certain how the practice of exchanging gifts and greeting cards on Valentine's Day began. It may have started with the Romans. At a festival during February, unmarried women put their names in a container. Unmarried men drew out names to see who would be their sweetheart. By the 17th century, it was a popular custom to send handmade valentines. Today, we still celebrate love and friendship on Valentine's Day.

✏️ Draw the type of valentine you would like to receive on the back of this page.

Seasonal Activities • EMC 2004 • © Evan-Moor Corp.

Name _____

Valentine Messages

Use the code to solve the riddles.

A = 26   G = 20   L = 15   Q = 10   V = 5
B = 25   H = 19   M = 14   R = 9   W = 4
C = 24   I = 18   N = 13   S = 8   X = 3
D = 23   J = 17   O = 12   T = 7   Y = 2
E = 22   K = 16   P = 11   U = 6   Z = 1
F = 21

What did the pig write to his sweetheart?

| __ | __ | __ | __ | | __ | __ | __ | | __ | __ | __ | __ | __ | __ |
| 19 | 12 | 20 | 8 | | 26 | 13 | 23 | | 16 | 18 | 8 | 8 | 22 | 8 |

What did the owl write to her sweetheart?

| __ | __ | __ | | __ | __ | __ | __ | __ | __ | | __ | __ |
| 12 | 4 | 15 | | 26 | 15 | 4 | 26 | 2 | 8 | | 25 | 22 |

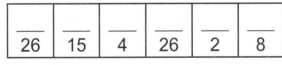

| __ | __ | __ | __ | | __ | __ | __ | __ | __ | __ | __ | __ |
| 2 | 12 | 6 | 9 | | 5 | 26 | 15 | 22 | 13 | 7 | 18 | 13 | 22 |

What did the bee say to his sweetheart?

| __ | __ | __ , | __ | __ | | __ | | __ | __ | __ | __ | __ |
| 2 | 12 | 6 | 9 | 22 | | 26 | | 19 | 12 | 13 | 22 | 2 |

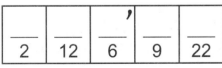

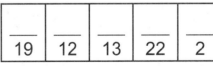

| __ | __ | | __ | | __ | __ | __ | __ | __ | __ | __ | __ | __ |
| 12 | 21 | | 26 | | 5 | 26 | 15 | 22 | 13 | 7 | 18 | 13 | 22 |

What would you write to your sweetheart? Write the message in code.

_____

_____

Name _____

February Fun Word Search

Find words about February holidays hidden in this puzzle.

```
P C U P I D R E W O L F W
R C A V S O T H U G I E A
E A B R A H A M G R N B S
S N I P D L A E G I C R H
I D R R S E D L N O U I I
D Y T E Y M L N O X L A N
E E H S A I Z O T W N R G
N S D E D L O E V I Q Y T
T O A N I E F R I E N D O
S R Y T L C G E O R G E N
I X G R O U N D H O G Z U
S E E C H E A R T S B Y E
D A I S Y F U N K W I N D
```

Word Box

Abraham	friend	love
birthday	fun	present
candy	George	presidents
cards	grin	rose
cupid	groundhog	shadow
daisy	heart	smile
February	holidays	valentine
flower	hug	Washington
	Lincoln	

Seasonal Activities • EMC 2004 • © Evan-Moor Corp.

Name _____

Eid al-Fitr

Read about Eid al-Fitr and then answer the questions.
Count by 2s to complete the mosque.

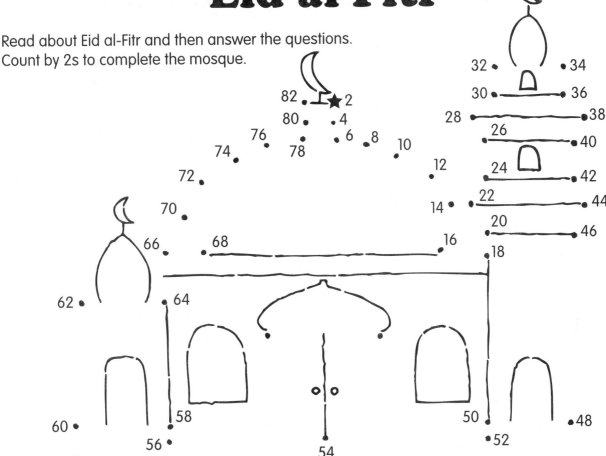

Eid al-Fitr is a joyous festival celebrated by Muslims. Muslims are followers of the faith of Islam. It is the "Feast of the Breaking of the Fast." It occurs at the end of Ramadan, a month-long time of fasting. (During Ramadan, Muslims do not eat from a half hour before dawn until sunset.)

On the morning of Eid al-Fitr, Muslims go to the mosque to pray. A special charity offering is given. People dress in holiday clothing and visit friends and relatives. Special meals are enjoyed. In some places, children are given small gifts of money.

1. Who celebrates Eid al-Fitr? _____

2. When is it celebrated? _____

3. Does your family celebrate Eid al-Fitr? _____

    If yes, how do you celebrate? _____

_____

Name _____

Tet Nguyen Dan

Read about Tet and then answer the questions.

The Vietnamese celebration Tet Nguyen Dan begins on the first day of the first month of the lunar new year. It is the largest celebration of the year. It is like New Year's, Thanksgiving, Fourth of July, and a birthday party for everyone all in one holiday. The holiday lasts three days.

The house is cleaned, food is prepared, and new clothes are bought. Family members return home to visit. Gifts are given at Tet. Children receive money in red envelopes. People enjoy fireworks, sporting events, concerts, dragon dancing, and singing.

1. How do the Vietnamese get ready for Tet? _____

_____

2. Describe one way Tet is celebrated. _____

_____

3. Does your family celebrate Tet? _____

   If yes, how do you celebrate? _____

_____

Name —————————————————————————

Name It

Write a word beginning with a letter in **spring** under each category.

	a flower	something you can buy in a store	something to eat or drink	an adjective (describing word)	a boy's name
Example ▷ L	lily	lock	lemonade	lumpy	Larry
S					
P					
R					
I					
N					
G					

84 **Spring**   Seasonal Activities • EMC 2004 • © Evan-Moor Corp.

Name _____

First Day of Spring

Read the paragraph and then answer the questions.

In the Northern Hemisphere, the first day of spring is usually March 21. (In the Southern Hemisphere, it is usually September 22.) It is called the Vernal Equinox. The Vernal Equinox is one of two times in the year when day and night are about the same length. The earth begins to warm up. It is a time of "rebirth," when plants sprout and many animals give birth to their young.

1. When is the first day of spring in the Northern Hemisphere? _____

2. What types of changes occur during spring?

   _____

   _____

3. What do you like best about spring?

   _____

   _____

   _____

Name ————————————————————

March Winds

Complete the crossword puzzle with "wind" words.

Across

1. a ship with sails
3. a machine that generates power using the wind
4. moving air
5. an unexpected lucky event or unexpected money

Down

1. the tube connecting the throat and lungs; the trachea

2. a person who says nothing interesting or important

3. a sheet of glass in front of the driver and riders in a vehicle

Word Box

wind
windbag
windfall
windjammer
windmill
windpipe
windshield

Name _____

In Like a Lion,
Out Like a Lamb

It is sometimes said that if the month of March comes "in like a lion" it will go "out like a lamb."
What do you think that means?

In like a lion:

_____

_____

_____

Out like a lamb:

_____

_____

_____

Label the pictures below: **in like a lion**   or   **out like a lamb**

_____   _____

Name _____

April Showers

Count by 3s. Then use the code to answer to the riddle about rainy April days.

a _____   i _____   r _____

b _____   k _____   s _____

c _____   l _____   t _____

d _____   n _____   u _____

e _____   o _____   v _____

h _____   p _____   y _____

Why don't mother kangaroos like April showers?

___ ___ ___ ___   ___ ___ ___   ___ ___ ___
6 15 9 3   48 42 15   45 18 15

___ ___ ___ ___   ___ ___ ___ ___   ___ ___
24 21 12 42   18 3 51 15   45 33

___ ___ ___ ___   ___ ___ ___ ___ ___ ___
36 27 3 54   21 30 12 33 33 39 42

Seasonal Activities • EMC 2004 • © Evan-Moor Corp.

March Winds and April Showers

Find the hidden weather words.

```
S U N S H I N E A W I N D B
W C O X W F P N X E P F R Q
E P R E C I P I T A T I O N
D D T E M P E R A T U R E G
M M S T O R M K Y H Z E S R
L I G H T N I N G E I O Q A
B B S D O E W O L R R G T I
R H L T R W G W U H T C H N
E M A R K I E J D E T L U D
E R A I N T P R N A D O N R
Z L G C L D V S S T U U D O
E Z H A C H E R Z S T D E P
I K L M O I S T U R E Y R S
```

Word Box

breeze	heat	mist	raindrops	temperature
cloudy	high	moisture	showers	thunder
dew	lightning	precipitation	storm	weather
drips	low	rain	sunshine	wind
fog				

Name _____

May Flowers

Write the flower names in alphabetical order.

buttercup	petunia	azalea
daffodil	orchid	carnation
honeysuckle	nasturtium	larkspur
violet	aster	zinnia
snapdragon	crocus	jasmine
marigold	daisy	begonia
hollyhock	lily	iris
rose	tulip	sweet pea

1. _____
2. _____
3. _____
4. _____
5. _____
6. _____
7. _____
8. _____
9. _____
10. _____
11. _____
12. _____

13. _____
14. _____
15. _____
16. _____
17. _____
18. _____
19. _____
20. _____
21. _____
22. _____
23. _____
24. _____

List your four favorite flowers here.

1. _____
2. _____

3. _____
4. _____

Name _____

Johnny Appleseed

Read about Johnny Appleseed and then answer the question.

John Chapman was a tree farmer. In the 1800s, he set out to explore the Northwest Territory. As he wandered, he carried a bag of apple seeds on his back. When he found a good spot, he would clear the land and plant apple trees. People began to call him "Johnny Appleseed."

As time went by, he became a folk hero. Many things people say he did were probably imaginary. But we do know that he planted a large number of apple trees on the early frontier.

How did John Chapman earn his nickname? _____

_____

_____

_____

Name _____

Johnny Appleseed's Favorite Snack

Plot the pairs of numbers on the graph in the order they are listed. Count across and then up.
Connect the points with straight lines. Start each new set of points with a new line.

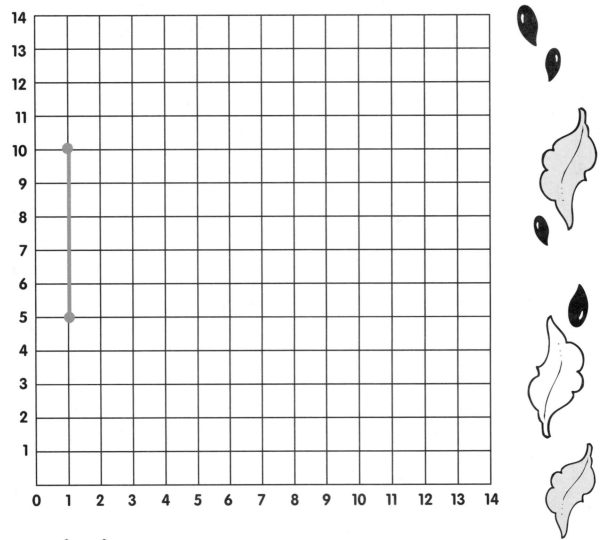

- (1,5) (1,10) (2,11) (5,11) (6,10) (7,11) (10,11) (11,10) (11,5) (10,3)
  (8,2) (7,2) (6,3) (5,2) (4,2) (2,3) (1,5) end of line

- (6,10) (5,12) (4,13) (7,13) (7,11) end of line

- (7,12) (8,13) (10,13) (7,11) end of line

An _____ a day keeps the doctor away.

Apple Treats

Do you think Johnny Appleseed imagined all of the ways people would find to use apples? Maddie found that her classmates enjoyed apples in many different ways. She recorded their favorites on a chart. Use the information on her chart to make a bar graph. Then answer the questions.

Ways to Eat Apples

raw apple	applesauce	apple pie	apple jelly	candied apple	apple fritters
13	4	9	10	8	5

	raw apple	applesauce	apple pie	apple jelly	candied apple	apple fritters
14						
12						
10						
8						
6						
4						
2						
0						

1. What is the difference between the most favorite way to eat apples

   and the least favorite way? _____

2. What is your favorite way to eat apples? _____

   _____

Name _____

The Tree Planter

Draw a line to guide Johnny Appleseed through the woods to the cabin.

Seasonal Activities • EMC 2004 • © Evan-Moor Corp.

Saint Patrick's Day

Read about Saint Patrick's Day and then answer the questions.

Do you have to be Irish to enjoy Saint Patrick's Day? Not at all. It can still be fun to celebrate all things "Irish." Dress in green, join in a parade, eat corned beef, and search for a leprechaun's treasure.

In Ireland, and for Catholics around the world, Saint Patrick's Day is a religious holiday. It honors a Christian missionary to Ireland in the fifth century A.D. When Patrick was 16 years old, he was kidnapped and sold into slavery in Ireland. After six years, he escaped. At the age of sixty, he was sent back to Ireland to preach about Christianity to the Irish. He remained in Ireland for a total of thirty years. March 17, the day of his death, has been celebrated as Saint Patrick's Day ever since.

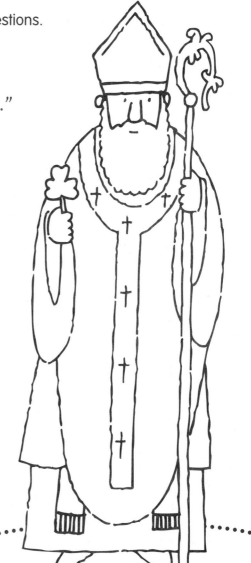

1. Who was Saint Patrick? _____

2. Why was he sent back to Ireland? _____

   _____

3. Does your family celebrate Saint Patrick's Day?_____

   If yes, how do you celebrate? _____

   _____

Name ————————————————————

Leprechauns

Read about leprechauns and then answer the question.
Draw the other side of the leprechaun.

A leprechaun is a type of Irish fairy. Leprechauns are said to be mean and spiteful. They are also said to be rich. Look carefully under mushrooms or in fields of clover, and you might catch one. If you do, he might offer you his pot of gold if you'll release him. Keep a close eye on the leprechaun, or he will vanish without paying you!

Give three reasons why you know leprechauns are not real.

1. _____

2. _____

3. _____

   Seasonal Activities • EMC 2004 • © Evan-Moor Corp.

Name ——————————————————————

My Lucky Shamrock

A shamrock leaf has three parts. There is a myth that says if you find a shamrock leaf with **four** parts, it will bring you good luck.

Write a wish on each section of this "lucky" shamrock.

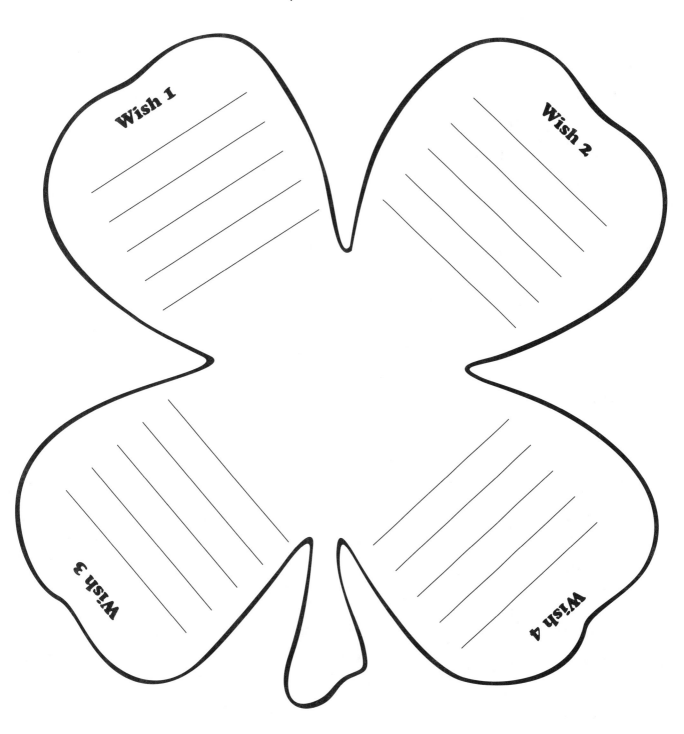

Wish 1

Wish 2

Wish 3

Wish 4

A Pot of Gold

Find 10 differences between these leprechauns.

1. _____

2. _____

3. _____

4. _____

5. _____

6. _____

7. _____

8. _____

9. _____

10. _____

 Seasonal Activities • EMC 2004 • © Evan-Moor Corp.

Saint Patrick's Day Word Search

Find the words hidden in the puzzle.

```
B Y S C A P T U R E N L E R
L S H I L L E L A G H E M A
A E A N L A S S W S O P E I
R E M I I V I R I S H R R N
N M R R N L E Y S L C E A B
E M O E T T A R H U A C L O
Y U C L O R P D E C T H D W
G S K A M E M A S K C A I C
U H E N G A T A T O H U S A
R R D D R S G I R R E N L B
G O I X E U X I N C I E E B
L O H M E R I N C Y H C W A
E M L A N E P O T A T O K G
T O A D S T O O L H U N T E
```

Word Box

blarney	Ireland	rainbow
cabbage	Irish	Saint Patrick
capture	lad	shamrock
catch	lass	shillelagh
Emerald Isle	leprechaun	silver
Erin	luck	tiny
gold	magic	toadstool
green	March	treasure
hide	mushroom	wee
hunt	potato	wishes

What Is It?

Use the code to find the answers.

A ⌐	G ⊏	N O	U ⊡
B ⌐	H ⊐	O ⌐·	V ⊡
C ⌐	I □	P ⌐·	W ⊡
D ⌐	J ⊏	Q ⌐·	X ⊙
E ⊔	K ⊔	R ·⌐	Y ⊍
F ⊓	L ⊔	S ⊡	Z ⊍
	M ⊍	T ⊡	

a tricky Irish elf

⸺⸺⸺⸺⸺⸺⸺⸺⸺⸺⸺⸺
∩ ⊔ ⌐ ⌐· ⊓ ⌐ ⊏ ⌐ ⊡ O

"lucky" green leaves

⸺⸺⸺⸺⸺⸺⸺⸺⸺⸺
⊡ ⊏ ⌐ ⊍ ⌐· ⌐ ⌐ ⊍ ⊡

vegetables with "eyes"

⸺⸺⸺⸺⸺⸺⸺⸺⸺⸺
⌐· ⌐· ⌐· ⊡ ⊡ ⌐· ⌐· ⊡ ·

a nickname for Ireland

⸺⸺⸺⸺⸺⸺⸺⸺   ⸺⸺⸺⸺
⊔ ⊍ ⊔ ⌐· ⌐ ⊔ ⌐   □ ⊡ ∩ ⊔

a kind of Irish talk that flatters you

⸺⸺⸺⸺⸺⸺⸺⸺⸺
⊔ ∩ ⊔ ⌐ ⌐ O ⊔ ⊍

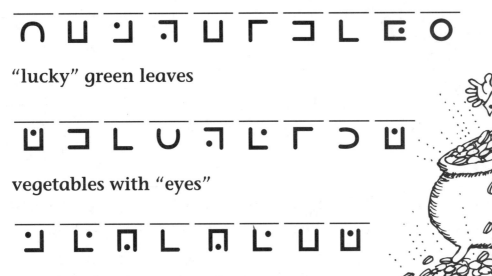

Seasonal Activities • EMC 2004 • © Evan-Moor Corp.

Name _____

Earth Day

Read about Earth Day and then answer the questions.

reduce the amount of garbage you throw away

reuse things instead of throwing them away

recycle cans and bottles

Reduce

Reuse

Recycle

Water

Soda

Recycling Bin

On April 22, 1970, the first Earth Day was held. The day was set aside for everyone to think about ways to take care of our Earth and its resources.

How clean is the air we breathe? How about the water we drink? How can we use the Earth's resources wisely? What can we do to protect the Earth's resources? These are just a few of the questions to think about on Earth Day.

What are some ways you take care of the Earth? _____

_____

_____

Name _____

Earth Day Word Search

Find the words hidden in the puzzle.

```
C L E A N A N I M A L S R
A C A R E E X T I N C T W
R I N E W N A Q L M P T O
E X R U A E M R I C E E R
C O N S E R V A T I O N L
Y X F E E G S P T H P O D
C Y Z U R Y O M E L L Z W
L G S S E R I M R X E O A
E E A P O L L U T I O N T
E N V I R O N M E N T E E
S E E V O L U N T E E R R
E C U D E R N O W P L E H
```

Word Box

air	Earth	litter	recycle	volunteer
animals	energy	oxygen	reduce	water
care	environment	ozone	reuse	world
clean	extinct	people	save	
conservation	fuel	pollution	soil	

Seasonal Activities • EMC 2004 • © Evan-Moor Corp.

Arbor Day

Name _____

Read about Arbor Day and then complete the word search.

Arbor Day was started in 1872. It is a day to honor and plant trees. On April 10, 1872, Arbor Day was first celebrated in Nebraska with the planting of over one million trees. Arbor Day is celebrated in different states on different days, but it is usually near April 22.

Trees provide us with many useful products. See how many you can find in the word search.

```
O  X  Y  G  E  N  I  C  E  M  Q  T
P  C  B  F  L  Y  P  A  P  E  R  U
L  O  O  U  R  S  T  U  N  D  E  R
Y  C  G  R  U  U  S  A  C  I  M  P
W  O  L  N  K  N  I  N  I  C  A  E
O  N  A  I  R  O  N  T  N  I  P  N
O  U  S  T  D  O  O  W  N  N  L  T
D  T  L  U  M  B  E  R  A  E  E  I
C  H  A  R  C  O  A  L  M  L  S  N
P  A  P  E  R  N  O  T  O  M  Y  E
R  O  O  T  R  E  S  I  N  S  R  B
C  H  E  W  I  N  G  G  U  M  U  U
B  X  T  C  I  D  E  R  A  M  P  G
C  A  R  D  B  O  A  R  D  X  P  S
```

Word Box

cardboard	coconut	lumber	paper
charcoal	cork	maple syrup	plywood
chewing gum	flypaper	medicine	resin
cider	fruit	nuts	turpentine
cinnamon	furniture	oxygen	wood

Name _____

Arbor Day Crossword Puzzle

Use the clues to complete the crossword puzzle.

Word Box

Arbor Day
bark
carbon dioxide
crown
deciduous
evergreen
leaves
limb
nuts
oxygen
roots

Across

1. the food-making part of a tree
3. trees that drop their leaves in the winter
7. the outer covering of a tree's trunk
9. trees absorb this, which helps clean the air
11. tree seeds that people eat

Down

2. a special day to celebrate trees
4. trees that remain green all year
5. another name for a tree branch
6. tree leaves release this into the air
8. the branches and leaves of a tree form a ____
10. these absorb water from the soil

Name _____

Tree Alphabet

Write the tree names in alphabetical order.

beech	ginko	eucalyptus	holly	pine
apple	yew	oak	quince	maple
fir	laurel	fig	locust	walnut
willow	dogwood	juniper	redbud	orange
cedar	spruce	palm	sycamore	birch
elm				

1. _____   14. _____

2. _____   15. _____

3. _____   16. _____

4. _____   17. _____

5. _____   18. _____

6. _____   19. _____

7. _____   20. _____

8. _____   21. _____

9. _____   22. _____

10. _____   23. _____

11. _____   24. _____

12. _____   25. _____

13. _____   26. _____

Circle the letters that are <u>not</u> used in your tree alphabet.

a b c d e f g h i j k l m n

o p q r s t u v w x y z

Name _____

Easter

Read about Easter and then answer the questions.
Draw a line to lead the family to church on Easter Sunday.

Easter is one of the most important religious holidays of the year for Christians. It is a time of joy, with special church services and festive meals.

1. Who celebrates Easter as a religious holiday?_____

2. Is Easter a religious celebration for your family? _____

   If yes, how do you celebrate? _____

   _____

Seasonal Activities • EMC 2004 • © Evan-Moor Corp.

Easter Fun

Children of all ages enjoy waking up Easter morning to find a basket filled with candy eggs and chocolate rabbits.

Draw the other side of the basket. Fill the basket.

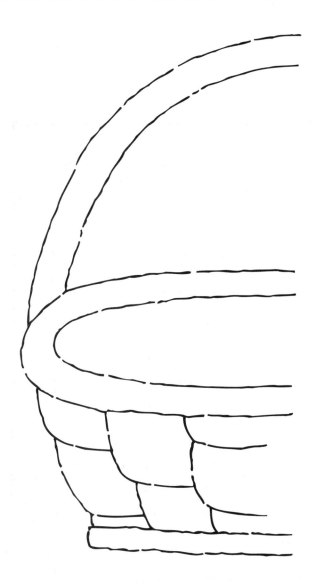

What would you like to find in your basket on Easter morning? Explain why.

_____

_____

_____

_____

Pysanky Eggs

Ukrainian Easter eggs are decorated with symbols of good wishes. These beautiful eggs are then given to special friends and family members. Here are some of the symbols used and what they mean:

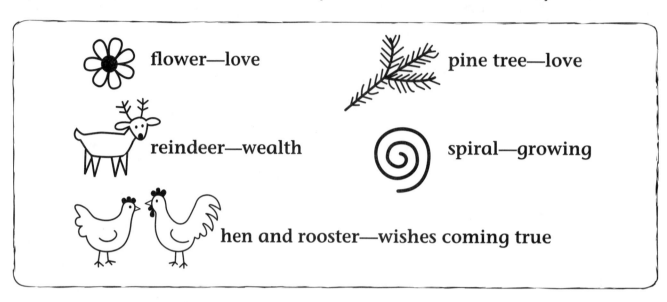

flower—love

pine tree—love

reindeer—wealth

spiral—growing

hen and rooster—wishes coming true

Decorate this egg with an "Easter wish." Give your egg to a special friend.

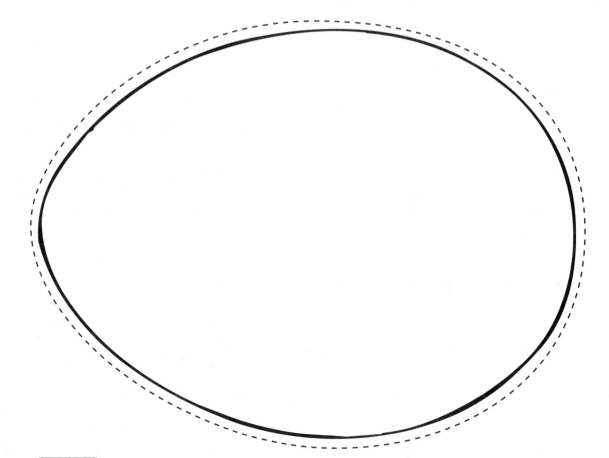

Name _____

An Eggs...tra Special Word Search

Find the types of eggs hidden in the word search.

```
N  S  C  R  A  M  B  L  E  D  G  E  B  E
O  A  G  M  A  E  G  G  E  G  G  G  O  G
O  N  G  E  R  W  E  G  G  P  E  G  I  F
D  D  E  G  D  R  O  P  S  O  U  P  L  F
L  W  E  G  G  Y  O  Z  E  A  S  T  E  R
E  I  D  E  G  G  E  L  X  C  A  E  D  I
S  C  U  S  T  A  R  D  L  H  L  E  E  E
C  H  O  C  O  L  A  T  E  E  A  G  G  D
E  G  G  S  T  U  F  F  E  D  D  E  G  G
```

Egg _____	
drop soup	custard
salad	roll
sandwich	noodles

_____ **eggs**		
raw	poached	Easter
scrambled	boiled	chocolate
fried	stuffed	dyed

Now...how many times can you find **egg** in the word search? _____

Easter Rabbit Riddles

Count by 6s and then use the code to solve the riddles

a _____   g _____   m _____   s _____

b _____   h _____   n _____   t _____

c _____   i _____   o _____   u _____

d _____   k _____   r _____   y _____

e _____   l _____

Why did the Easter Rabbit cross the road?

___ ___ ___   ___ ___ ___ ___ ___ ___
96 42 30   18 42 48 18 54 30 72

___ ___ ___   ___ ___ ___
42   6 24   42 48 90

___ ___ ___ ___ ___ ___   ___ ___ ___ ___
30   6 90 96 30 84   30 36 36 90

What is the best way to send a letter to the Easter Rabbit?

___ ___   ___ ___ ___ ___   ___ ___ ___ ___
12 108   42   6 84 30   66   6 48 60

What do you get if you pour hot water down the Easter Rabbit's hole?

___   ___ ___ ___   ___ ___ ___ ___ ___
6   42 78 96   18 84 78 90 90

___ ___ ___ ___ ___
12 102 72 72 108

What Is It?

Plot the pairs of numbers on the graph in the order they are listed. Count across and then up. Connect the points with straight lines. Start each new set of points with a new line.

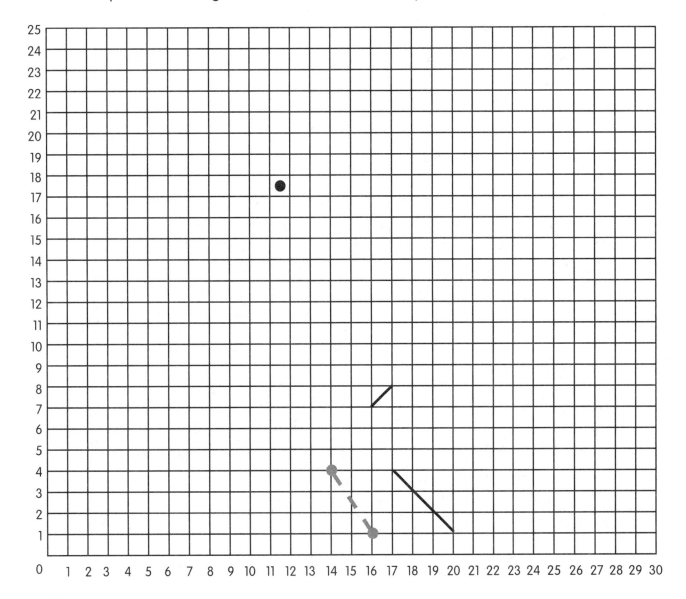

- (16,1) (14,4) (16,7) (14,9) (14,7) (12,9) (14,11) (14,15) (10,15) (10,17) (12,19) (13,19) (16,23) (18,24) (15,19) (15,16) (18,13) (22,9) (24,6) (26,7) (26,3) (24,3) (22,1) (20,1) (16,1) line ends

- (4,2) (2,6) (2,8) (4,10) (7,10) (9,8) (9,6) (7,2) (4,2) line ends

- (3,6) (3,8) (4,9) (7,9) (8,8) (8,6) (3,6) line ends

Name _____

Cinco de Mayo

Read about Cinco de Mayo and then answer the questions.

Cinco de Mayo means the "fifth of May." It is an important holiday in Mexico. It celebrates the victory of a group of Mexicans over invading French soldiers at the battle of Puebla on May 5, 1862. Cinco de Mayo is a day to remember the courage of those Mexican peasants.

The celebration of Cinco de Mayo includes parades, mock battles, dances, fireworks, and flower festivals. Many Mexican people living in the United States also celebrate this holiday.

1. What is the meaning of Cinco de Mayo? _____

_____

2. Why was the battle of Puebla fought? _____

_____

3. Does your family celebrate Cinco de Mayo? _____

   If yes, how do you celebrate? _____

_____

   Seasonal Activities • EMC 2004 • © Evan-Moor Corp.

Name —————————————

The Mexican Flag

Follow the directions to color the Mexican flag.

The left-hand panel of the flag stands for **hope**. It is green.

The right-hand panel of the flag stands for **union**. It is red.

The center panel is white. It stands for **purity**.

Describe the picture on the center panel.———————————

————————————————————————

————————————————————————

————————————————————————

Name _____

English to Spanish

Count by 3s to connect the dots.

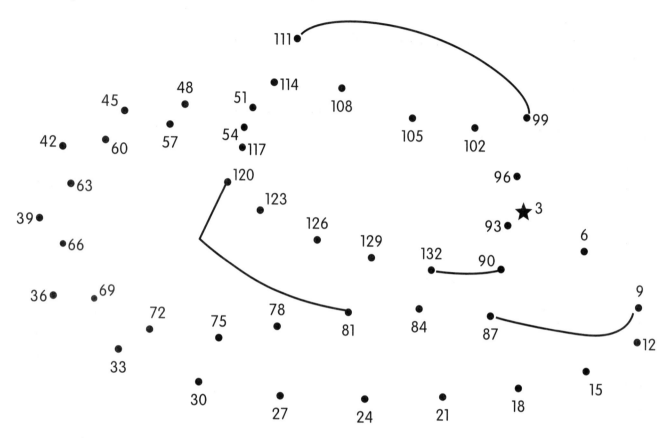

Match the English and Spanish words.

hat	Cinco de Mayo
fifth of May	amigo
friend	sombrero
yes	musica
celebration	si
music	gracias
thank you	por favor
please	celebración

What did you make? Write your answer in English and in Spanish.

_____   _____

                    Seasonal Activities • EMC 2004 • © Evan-Moor Corp.

Name _____

Mother's Day

In 1914, President Wilson proclaimed the second Sunday in May to be an official national holiday honoring mothers. It is also a day to honor all women who act as a mother figure in your life.

Draw a picture of your mother.

Write a list of 10 words that describe her.

1. _____   6. _____

2. _____   7. _____

3. _____   8. _____

4. _____   9. _____

5. _____   10. _____

Name _____

About My Mother

Interview your mother to find out the answers to these questions.

1. Where were you born?

   _____

2. Where did you go to school?

   _____

3. What was your favorite game when you were my age? Why?

   _____

4. What were you best at in school?

   _____

5. What is your best memory from childhood?

   _____

6. What do you like best about your job?

   _____

7. What is your favorite food? Why?

   _____

8. What is your favorite way to exercise?

   _____

9. Is there someplace in the world you would like to go for a special vacation? Why? _____

10. What do you like best about being a mother? _____

   _____

Seasonal Activities • EMC 2004 • © Evan-Moor Corp.

Name ———————————————————

Memorial Day

Read about Memorial Day and then answer the questions.

May 30 is Memorial Day. It is a day to remember the men and women who have died in service to our country. During the Civil War, women's groups in the South decorated soldiers' graves with flowers and flags. This custom continues today. Graves of soldiers are decorated with flowers, wreaths, or small flags.

At Arlington National Cemetery, an American flag is placed on each grave. The president or vice president places a wreath on the Tomb of the Unknown Soldier.

1. Whom does Memorial Day honor?

———————————————————————————————

2. Why do you think it is necessary to have a tomb dedicated to unknown

soldiers? —————————————————————————

———————————————————————————————

Memorial Day Crossword Puzzle

Complete the puzzle.

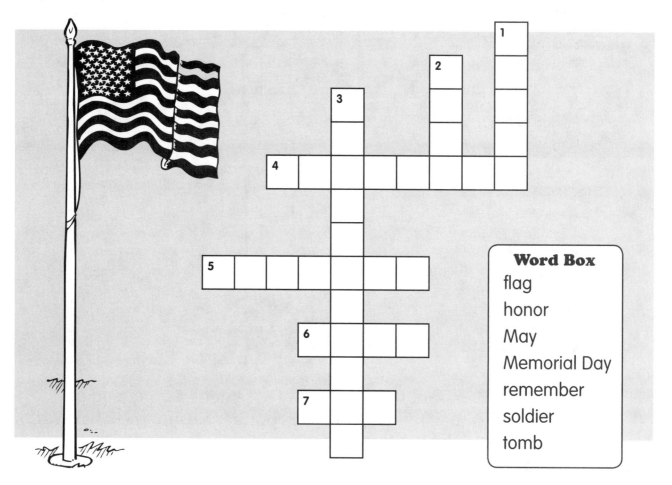

Word Box
flag
honor
May
Memorial Day
remember
soldier
tomb

Across

4. to recall something that happened in the past

5. someone serving in the Army

6. the "Stars and Stripes"

7. the month in which Memorial Day takes place

Down

1. to hold in high regard; to show respect

2. the place where the unknown soldier is buried

3. the day on which we honor men and women who died in service for our country

Seasonal Activities • EMC 2004 • © Evan-Moor Corp.

Name It

Write a word beginning with a letter in **summer** under each category.

	a type of clothing	a city or country	an object in space	food or drink	a noun
Example P	pinafore	Paris	planet	peanut butter	pony
S					
U					
M					
M					
E					
R					

Summer Cinquain

Follow the steps to write a cinquain about summer.

_____

Line 1 one-word title

_____

Line 2 two words about the title

_____

Line 3 three words describing an action

_____

Line 4 four words describing a feeling

_____

Line 5 one-word synonym for the title (or repeat the title)

Now illustrate your poem.

Name _____

How to Stay Cool in the Summertime

List the ways to stay cool on a hot summer day.

1. _____
2. _____
3. _____
4. _____
5. _____
6. _____
7. _____
8. _____
9. _____
10. _____

Illustrate one of your ideas on the back of this page.

Sun Fun

Complete the crossword puzzle.
All of the answers contain the word **sun**.

Across

1. sore red skin from too much sun

2. a type of hat worn by pioneer women to protect them from the sun

3. when the sun disappears below the horizon

4. when the sun appears over the horizon

6. the first day of the week

Down

1. a tall plant with large yellow flowers and edible seeds

2. rays of sunlight

4. the star nearest the Earth

5. an outdoor device that shows the time by shadows on a dial

Name _____

Then and Now

Read about the United States flag and then answer the question.

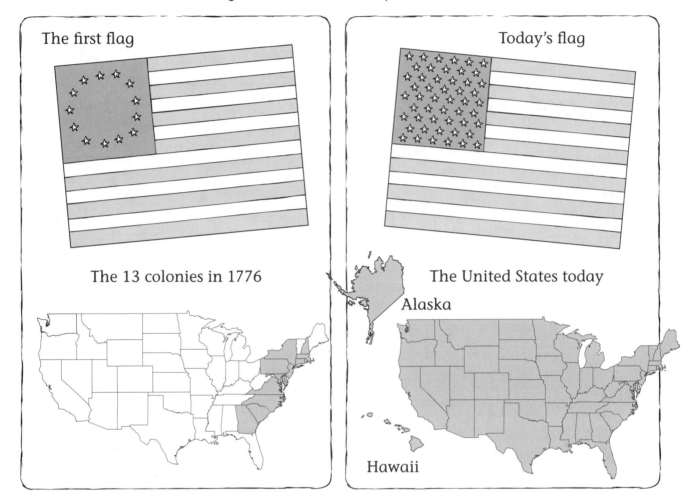

The first flag

Today's flag

The 13 colonies in 1776

The United States today

Alaska

Hawaii

The original flag represented the first 13 colonies in two ways—13 stars and 13 stripes. As the country grew, another star and stripe were added for each new state. This soon became a problem. There were too many new states to keep adding all of those stripes!

So the stripes remain at 13 to represent the first 13 states, and a star has been added for each new state. Since 1959, when Hawaii and Alaska became states, the number of stars has remained at 50.

How has the flag changed since 1777? _____

_____

_____

Name _____

Red, White, and Blue

The United States is not the only country with a red, white, and blue flag. Color each of these flags, which are only a few examples. (**r**—red, **b**—blue, **w**—white) Use the code to name each country.

a-26	**g**-20	**l**-15	**q**-10	**v**-5
b-25	**h**-19	**m**-14	**r**-9	**w**-4
c-24	**i**-18	**n**-13	**s**-8	**x**-3
d-23	**j**-17	**o**-12	**t**-7	**y**-2
e-22	**k**-16	**p**-11	**u**-6	**z**-1
f-21				

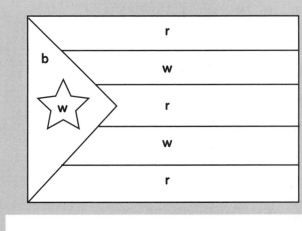

___ ___ ___ ___ ___ ___ ___ ___ ___ ___
11 6 22 9 7 12 9 18 24 12

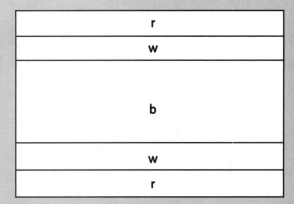

___ ___ ___ ___ ___ ___ ___ ___
7 19 26 18 15 26 13 23

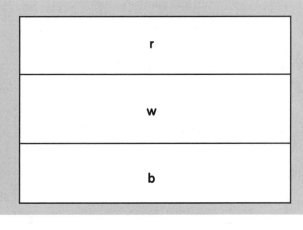

___ ___ ___ ___ ___ ___ ___ ___ ___ ___ ___
13 22 7 19 22 9 15 26 13 23 8

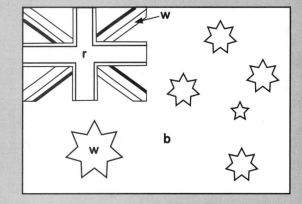

___ ___ ___ ___ ___ ___ ___ ___ ___
26 6 8 7 9 26 15 18 26

Name _____

The First U.S. Flag

The first flag of the United States had 13 stars and 13 stripes—
one star and one stripe for each of the original states.

Find the 13 original states in the word search.

```
N Z R E D L H K H N R E A S P
E O Z H Q E R A E D R S I O C
W P R K O O L W C I V L N U O
J N P T Y D J A H W H X I T N
E A E W H E E S W U P B G H N
R P E W R C P I B A V Y R C E
S N L S Y M A C S K R K I A C
E C E X A O L R V L K E V R T
Y Y Z H E Z R B O G A B E O I
B A W O L D F K H L U N F L C
L E M A R Y L A N D I T D I U
N G E O R G I A W Z M N Y N T
N E W H A M P S H I R E A A R
M A S S A C H U S E T T S U I
P E N N S Y L V A N I A V X C
```

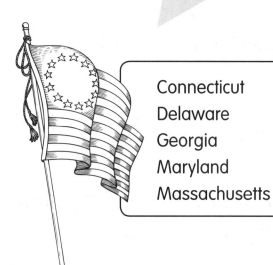

Word Box

Connecticut	New Hampshire	Pennsylvania
Delaware	New Jersey	Rhode Island
Georgia	New York	South Carolina
Maryland	North Carolina	Virginia
Massachusetts		

Seasonal Activities • EMC 2004 • © Evan-Moor Corp.

Name _____

Pledge of Allegiance

I pledge allegiance to the flag
of the United States of America
and to the republic for which it stands,
one nation under God, indivisible,
with liberty and justice for all.

The pledge of allegiance contains some difficult words.
See if you can match each of these words with its meaning.

pledge ★   loyalty to a government, cause, or
                            person

allegiance ★
                            a group of people living in a particular
                            area under a central government

republic ★
                            a solemn promise

nation ★
                            cannot be divided

indivisible ★   freedom from the control of others

justice ★   a government where power is given to
                            officials elected by the people

liberty ★   fairness according to principles of right
                            and wrong

Name _____

Flag Day

Read about Flag Day and then answer the questions.

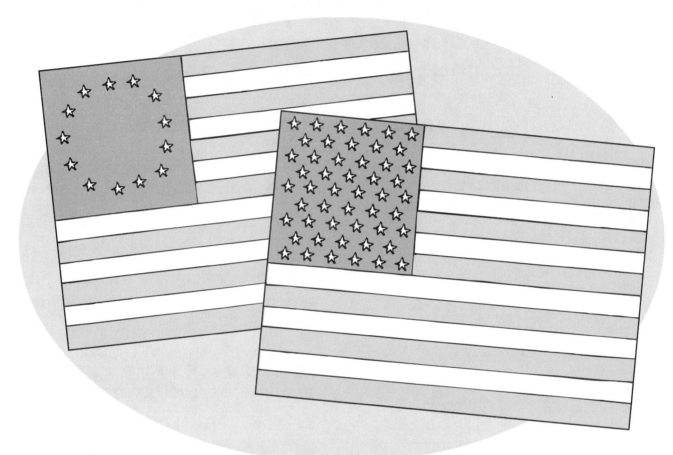

 Did you know the U.S. flag has two names? It is called the
"Stars and Stripes." It is also called "Old Glory." No matter what
you call it, the flag stands for the United States of America.

 The first U.S. flag had seven red and six white stripes with 13 white
stars on a blue background. It became the official U.S. flag on June 14,
1777. Today, June 14 is celebrated as Flag Day with flying flags and
patriotic speeches.

1. What are the two nicknames for the U.S. flag?

_____   _____

2. Describe the first U.S. flag.

_____

_____

Seasonal Activities • EMC 2004 • © Evan-Moor Corp.

Name _____

Betsy Ross and the 5-Pointed Star

Read about Betsy Ross and then answer the questions.

In 1776, the United States was a new country. It needed a new flag. According to popular legend, George Washington and two other men visited a seamstress named Betsy Ross. They showed her a drawing of the flag they wanted. It had stripes and six-pointed stars. Betsy Ross thought a five-pointed star would look better. She showed the men how easy it was to make one. The men agreed that the five-pointed star should be on the flag.

In June 1977, Congress passed the Flag Resolution, making the "Stars and Stripes" the official flag of the United States.

1. What is the job of a seamstress? _____

_____

2. Why did George Washington want a new flag made? _____

_____

3. Circle the star above that you think looks best. Explain your choice.

_____

_____

Fun in the Sun Word Search

Find the words hidden in the puzzle.

```
S U M M E R V A C A T I O N C A M P F I R E
U U F A N P A R K G A P P Y S U T O I H S S
N J M R J U M P R O P E I B W G R O S I A W
S U I M I U X L F G L H C A I U I L H K N I
H N A C E E L A I U I O N S M S P X I E D M
I E W N E R N Y S I N O I K E T T E N T C S
N N O I T E T D H D E K C E E T I K G R A U
E S O C E A N I S E B A I T B A A T P A S I
F H D E S A I L M B A C K P A C K O O V T T
R O S C V B U S M E R S K H O O L P L E L H
I R B R A N O A N W E H O L I D A Y E L E A
S T I E N M U A O O F B A S E B A L L G O T
B S K A M A P G T R O T H E M E P A R K N T
E Q E M O V I E A M O S U N G L A S S E S O
E S A N D A L S N S T S W E A T B E A C H H
```

Word Box

August	fish	ice ceam	sandals	tan
backpack	fishing pole	July	sand castle	tent
bait	friends	jump rope	shorts	theme park
barefoot	Frisbee	June	summer	travel
baseball	fun	kite	summertime	trip
basket	guide	movie	sunglasses	vacation
beach	hat	ocean	sunshine	van
bike	hike	park	sweat	woods
boat	holiday	picnic	swim	worms
camp	hook	play	swimsuit	
campfire	hot	pool		
fan	ice	sail		

Seasonal Activities • EMC 2004 • © Evan-Moor Corp.

Name _____

A Summer Picnic

Plan a picnic. Think about what you will eat and the games you will play.
Make lists of the things that you will need.

Menu	Games	Things to Bring
_____	_____	_____
_____	_____	_____
_____	_____	_____
_____	_____	_____
_____	_____	_____
_____	_____	_____
_____	_____	_____
_____	_____	_____

Write an invitation to send to one of your friends.
Tell when and where the picnic will take place.

You're Invited!

_____

_____

_____

_____

_____

Name _____

What I Did on Vacation

Think about a vacation you have taken and then answer the questions.

1. Where did you go?_____

_____

2. Did anyone go with you?_____

_____

3. How did you travel there? _____

_____

4. What did you take with you?_____

_____

5. What did you do when you got there? _____

_____

6. What was the best part of the vacation? _____

_____

7. What was the worst part of the vacation? _____

_____

8. What did you bring home for a souvenir? _____

_____

Turn the page over and illustrate one part of your vacation.

                    Seasonal Activities • EMC 2004 • © Evan-Moor Corp.

Sailing, Sailing

Copy the sailboat onto the grid.

Summer winds blowing
White sails billowing
My boat skims over the sea.

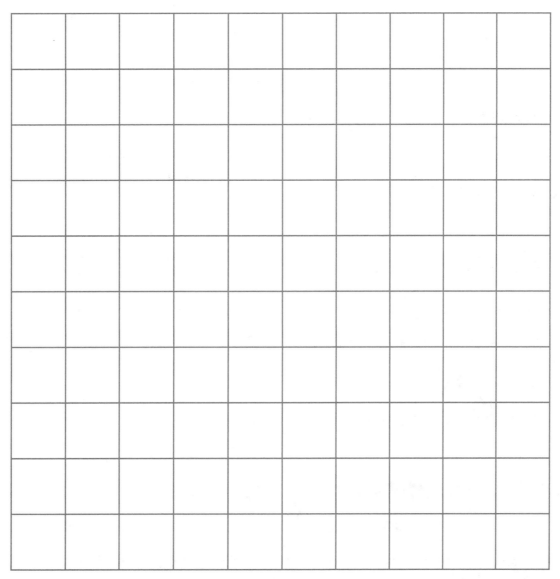

News from Camp

Write a friendly letter about exciting or disastrous things that might happen at summer camp.

_____

_____

_____

_____

_____

_____

_____

_____

_____

_____

_____

_____

_____

Seasonal Activities • EMC 2004 • © Evan-Moor Corp.

Name _____

Ways to Get There

Complete the chart to explain what you like and don't like about these different ways of travel.

Type of Vehicle	Its Advantages	Its Disadvantages

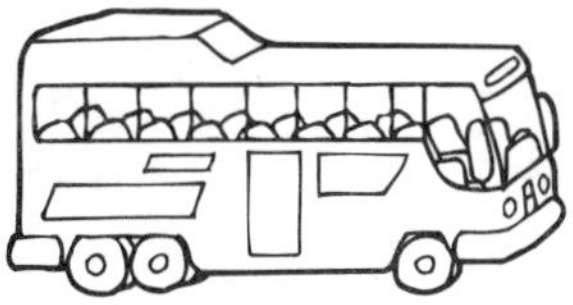		

✏️ Circle the ways you have traveled.

Touring North America

Use the code to find the names of these places to visit on vacation.

a-26	**g**-20	**m**-14	**s**-8	**w**-4
b-25	**h**-19	**n**-13	**t**-7	**x**-3
c-24	**i**-18	**o**-12	**u**-6	**y**-2
d-23	**j**-17	**p**-11	**v**-5	**z**-1
e-22	**k**-16	**q**-10		
f-21	**l**-15	**r**-9		

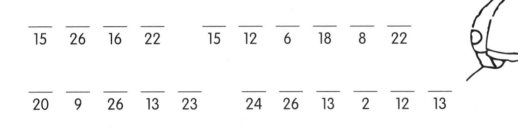

$\overline{15}\ \overline{26}\ \overline{16}\ \overline{22}\quad \overline{15}\ \overline{12}\ \overline{6}\ \overline{18}\ \overline{8}\ \overline{22}$

$\overline{20}\ \overline{9}\ \overline{26}\ \overline{13}\ \overline{23}\quad \overline{24}\ \overline{26}\ \overline{13}\ \overline{2}\ \overline{12}\ \overline{13}$

$\overline{13}\ \overline{22}\ \overline{4}\quad \overline{2}\ \overline{12}\ \overline{9}\ \overline{16}\quad \overline{24}\ \overline{18}\ \overline{7}\ \overline{2}$

$\overline{24}\ \overline{26}\ \overline{15}\ \overline{20}\ \overline{26}\ \overline{9}\ \overline{2}$

$\overline{9}\ \overline{12}\ \overline{24}\ \overline{16}\ \overline{2}\quad \overline{14}\ \overline{12}\ \overline{6}\ \overline{13}\ \overline{7}\ \overline{26}\ \overline{18}\ \overline{13}\ \overline{8}$

$\overline{19}\ \overline{26}\ \overline{4}\ \overline{26}\ \overline{18}\ \overline{18}$

$\overline{4}\ \overline{26}\ \overline{8}\ \overline{19}\ \overline{18}\ \overline{13}\ \overline{20}\ \overline{7}\ \overline{12}\ \overline{13}\ ,\ \overline{23}\ .\ \overline{24}\ .$

✏ Choose one place you would like to visit. Explain why on the back of this page.

Seasonal Activities • EMC 2004 • © Evan-Moor Corp.

Name _____

Summer Fun in
Your Own Backyard

Make a list of 8 ways to have fun at home.

1. _____
2. _____
3. _____
4. _____
5. _____
6. _____
7. _____
8. _____

Make a list of 4 ways to have fun around town.

1. _____
2. _____
3. _____
4. _____

National Parks

In 1872, Yellowstone became the first national park in the United States. It was established to protect the scenic land and to make it available for everyone to visit and enjoy. Today, there are national parks throughout the United States.

Find the national parks hidden in the word search.

```
M Y O S E M I T E R T B X
O E V E R G L A D E S A C
U L S Z Q M T B E B A D A
N L Y A I L C G N I G L N
T O A M V O H K A G U A Y
R W B S P E N R L B A N O
A S I V S I R W I E R D N
I T M N T E C D S N O S L
N O A L D X N Q E D F N A
I N B R Y C E C A N Y O N
E E H A L E A K A L A E D
R J Z U P Z W V D I O Y S
Q R G R A N D T E T O N P
R O C K Y M O U N T A I N
```

Word Box

Badlands	Grand Teton	Rocky Mountain
Big Bend	Haleakala	Saguaro
Bryce Canyon	Lassen	Wind Cave
Canyonlands	Mesa Verde	Yellowstone
Denali	Mount Rainier	Yosemite
Everglades	Olympic	Zion

Seasonal Activities • EMC 2004 • © Evan-Moor Corp.

Complete the Face

Draw the other side of this face.

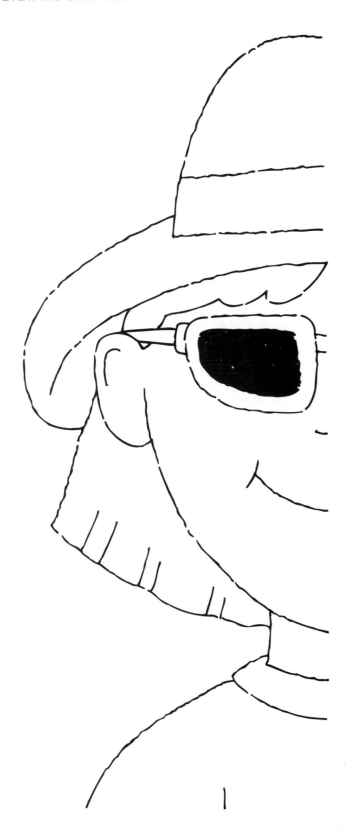

Name _____

Father's Day

Father's Day is one of our newest holidays. In 1966, President Lyndon Johnson signed a presidential proclamation declaring the third Sunday of June as Father's Day. It is a day to not only honor your father, but all men who act as a father figure in your life.

Draw a picture of your father.

Write a list of 10 words that describe him.

1. _____   6. _____

2. _____   7. _____

3. _____   8. _____

4. _____   9. _____

5. _____   10. _____

Name _____

About My Father

Interview your father to find out the answers to these questions.

1. Where were you born? _____

2. Where did you go to school?_____

3. What was your favorite game when you were my age? _____
   _____

4. What were you best at in school?_____

5. What is your best memory from childhood? _____
   _____
   _____

6. What do you like best about your job? _____
   _____
   _____

7. What is your favorite food? _____

8. What is your favorite way to exercise? _____
   _____

9. Is there someplace in the world you would like to go for a special vacation?
   _____
   _____

10. What do you like best about being a father?_____
    _____
    _____

Independence Day USA

Independence Day is the greatest patriotic holiday in the United States. It is celebrated on the fourth of July, the day on which the Second Continental Congress signed the Declaration of Independence in 1776. The Declaration was read to the public in Philadelphia four days later and celebrated with ringing bells. Each year all across the United States, we celebrate July 4th with parades, picnics, band concerts, speeches, and fireworks.

Complete the crossword puzzle.

Seasonal Activities • EMC 2004 • © Evan-Moor Corp.

Across

2. explosive devices for making a display of bright lights high in the sky

4. freedom from control by others

6. the _____ is Independence Day in the United States

7. a public procession usually having marching bands and floats

9. sounds organized to have rhythm, melody, and harmony

10. festive activities for a special occasion

Down

1. marching _____ are musical groups in a parade

2. the power to determine your own actions without asking the permission of others

3. a form of communication spoken before an audience

5. vehicles carrying displays in a parade

6. pieces of cloth containing special colors or symbols to represent nations

8. you may carry lunch to the park in a _____ basket

Word Box

bands	floats	music
celebration	Fourth of July	parade
fireworks	freedom	picnic
flags	independence	speech

Name —————————————————

Symbols of the USA

Unscramble these names of symbols of the United States of America. Then draw a line to match each word to the correct symbol.

— — — — — — — —

— — — — —

bertyli lelb

— — — —

agfl

— — — —

— — — — —

dalb geael

— — — — — — — —

— — — — — — —

tatues fo tyberli

— — — — — — — —

eatgr leas

— — — — — —

— — — — —

hiwte eoush

Seasonal Activities • EMC 2004 • © Evan-Moor Corp.

Take a Close Look

Find ten differences between the Statues of Liberty.

1. _____   6. _____

2. _____   7. _____

3. _____   8. _____

4. _____   9. _____

5. _____   10. _____

Name _____

The Great Seal of the USA

Read about the Great Seal and
then answer the questions.

The Great Seal of the United States was created to serve as
an emblem for the United States.

In the center of the seal is our national bird, the bald eagle.
The eagle holds a scroll in its beak. The scroll says "e pluribus unum."
This means "out of many, one." It shows that we are one nation that
was created from many colonies. The Great Seal has many ways of
representing the first 13 states:

13 stars above the eagle's head   13 arrows in the eagle's left claw
13 stripes on the shield   13 olives and leaves in the eagle's right claw

The Great Seal is on display in Washington, D.C. It is also on
the back of the one-dollar bill.

1. What does "out of many, one" mean? _____

2. Why are there so many thirteens on the Great Seal? _____

_____

3. If you were designing a seal for the United States, what would you have

included? _____

_____

Seasonal Activities • EMC 2004 • © Evan-Moor Corp.

Answer Key

Page 3

First Day of Autumn

Read the paragraph and then answer the questions.

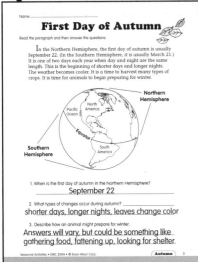

In the Northern Hemisphere, the first day of autumn is usually September 22. (In the Southern Hemisphere, it is usually March 21.) It is one of two days each year when day and night are the same length. This is the beginning of shorter days and longer nights. The weather becomes cooler. It is a time to harvest many types of crops. It is time for animals to begin preparing for winter.

1. When is the first day of autumn in the Northern Hemisphere?
September 22

2. What types of changes occur during autumn?
shorter days, longer nights, leaves change color

3. Describe how an animal might prepare for winter.
Answers will vary, but could be something like gathering food, fattening up, looking for shelter.

Page 4

Autumn Crossword Puzzle

Use the clues to solve the crossword puzzle.

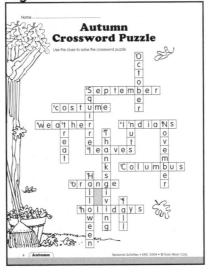

Page 6

Autumn Colors

Read the paragraph and then answer the questions.

Autumn is a time of change in many types of trees. They shed their green leaves. They put on a bright coat of fall leaves. How does this change happen?

During the spring and summer, leaves produce food for the tree. The part of the leaf that is used in this process contains chlorophyll. Chlorophyll gives the leaves their green color. Leaves also contain orange and yellow. These colors are hidden by the green.

As days grow shorter and colder, changes occur in the leaves. A thin layer of cells grows over the water tubes in the leaves. Now no water can get into the leaf. The leaves stop making food. The chlorophyll breaks down and the green color disappears. This allows the yellow and orange colors to be seen. Finally, the leaves die and fall from the tree.

Not all trees have leaves that change color. Evergreen trees such as pines, cedars, and firs stay green all year round. Their tough, needlelike leaves can survive winter's cold.

1. What gives leaves their green color? What is its job?
Chlorophyll.   It makes the leaves green.

2. What happens when the leaves can't get water?
They stop making food.

3. How do you think evergreens got their name?
They are always green.

Page 7

Autumn Word Search

Find the autumn words hidden in the word search. You will find words across, down, and diagonally.

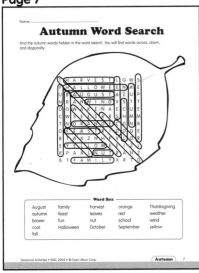

Word Box

August	family	harvest	orange	Thanksgiving
autumn	feast	leaves	red	weather
brown	fun	nut	school	wind
cool	Halloween	October	September	yellow
fall				

Page 9

School Days

Circle each word as you find it. You will find words across, down, and diagonally.

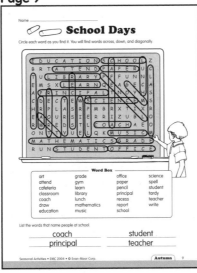

Word Box

art	grade	office	science
attend	gym	paper	spell
cafeteria	learn	pencil	student
classroom	library	principal	tardy
coach	lunch	recess	teacher
draw	mathematics	report	write
education	music	school	

List the words for people at school.
coach   student
principal   teacher

Page 11

Back-to-School Crossword Puzzle

Use the clues to complete the crossword puzzle.

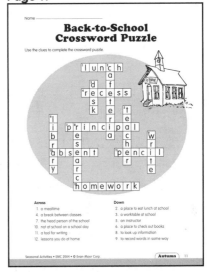

Across
1. a mealtime
4. a break between classes
7. the head person of the school
10. not at school on a school day
11. a tool for writing
12. lessons you do at home

Down
2. a place to eat lunch at school
3. a worktable at school
5. an instructor
6. a place to check out books
8. to look up information
9. to record words in some way

Page 12

Categories

Write the words in sets of things that go together. Give each set a title that explains how the items are alike.

Things in a classroom	People at school
title of set	*title of set*
1. books	1. coach
2. computer	2. librarian
3. paint	3. principal
4. paper	4. student
5. pencil	5. teacher

Places at school	Subjects at school
title of set	*title of set*
1. cafeteria	1. history
2. classroom	2. math
3. gym	3. music
4. library	4. reading
5. office	5. science

Word Box

books	gym	music	principal
cafeteria	history	office	reading
classroom	librarian	paint	science
coach	library	paper	student
computer	math	pencil	teacher

Page 13

Around School

Draw a line to show George's path to the school bus.

List in order the places he went on the way to the bus.
classroom   library   cafeteria

Page 14

Native American Day

Read the paragraph and then answer the questions.

By the time the first explorers and settlers arrived from Europe, Native Americans had lived throughout North America for thousands of years. There were at least 600 tribes of Native Americans in North America. Each tribe had its own heritage, customs, and values.

Native Americans are not just a part of the past. Two and a half million Native Americans representing 500 tribes still live in the United States and Canada. They live and work in cities, rural areas, and on reservations. As well as being a part of modern society, Native Americans take pride in reviving tribal traditions and customs.

Many states have set aside a day to honor and celebrate Native Americans and their cultures.

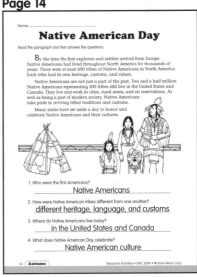

1. Who were the first Americans?
Native Americans

2. How were Native American tribes different from one another?
different heritage, language, and customs

3. Where do Native Americans live today?
in the United States and Canada

4. What does Native American Day celebrate?
Native American culture

Page 15

About Native Americans

Read and then answer the questions.

- In 1492, Christopher Columbus arrived and thought that he was in India. He called all of the tribes "Indians" even though these people were scattered all over the continent, spoke different languages, and had different customs.
- There were over 300 Native American nations, speaking 143 different languages and 1,000 dialects, living in North America when the colonists arrived.
- The Native Americans traded deerskin and beaver pelts for metal products and cloth made by the colonists. European explorers, fur traders, and colonists of the 1600s learned how to make white birch bark canoes from the Native Americans in the Northeast.
- The Iroquois League of Nations formed the powerful, united Great Council. Benjamin Franklin observed a council meeting to learn about their form of government.
- By the late 1800s, most Native Americans had been forced by the U.S. government to live on reservations. Many Native Americans still live on these reservations. They proudly hold onto their tribal customs and teach the history of their people to their children. Other Native Americans live in cities and towns across the United States.
- In 1924, all Native Americans in the United States were made citizens.

1. Why did Columbus call the Native Americans "Indians"?
   He thought he was in India.

2. Are all Native American tribes alike? Explain your answer.
   No, they have different heritage, language, and customs.

Seasonal Activities • EMC 2004 • © Evan-Moor Corp.   Autumn   15

Page 16

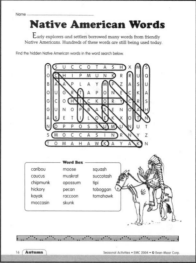

Native American Words

Early explorers and settlers borrowed many words from friendly Native Americans. Hundreds of these words are still being used today.

Find the hidden Native American words in the word search below.

Word Box

caribou	moose	squash
caucus	muskrat	succotash
chipmunk	opossum	tipi
hickory	pecan	toboggan
kayak	raccoon	tomahawk
moccasin	skunk	

16   Autumn   Seasonal Activities • EMC 2004 • © Evan-Moor Corp.

Page 18

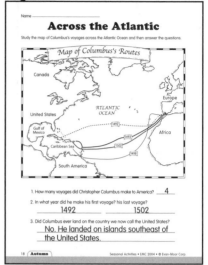

Across the Atlantic

Study the map of Columbus's voyages across the Atlantic Ocean and then answer the questions.

Map of Columbus's Routes

1. How many voyages did Christopher Columbus make to America?   4

2. In what year did he make his first voyage? his last voyage?
   1492   1502

3. Did Columbus ever land on the country we now call the United States?
   No. He landed on islands southeast of the United States.

18   Autumn   Seasonal Activities • EMC 2004 • © Evan-Moor Corp.

Page 19

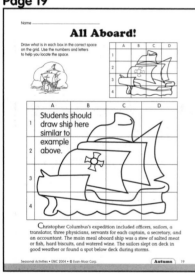

All Aboard!

Draw what is in each box in the correct space on the grid. Use the numbers and letters to help you locate the space.

Students should draw ship here similar to example above.

Christopher Columbus's expedition included officers, sailors, a translator, three physicians, servants for each captain, a secretary, and an accountant. The main meal aboard ship was a stew of salted meat or fish, hard biscuits, and watered wine. The sailors slept on deck in good weather or found a spot below deck during storms.

Seasonal Activities • EMC 2004 • © Evan-Moor Corp.   Autumn   19

Page 21

Take a Close Look

Find 10 differences between the two pictures.

1. dots on scarf
2. 2 ends on scarf
3. eye patch different
4. mustache
5. collar (line)
6. buttons
7. bird's eye
8. bird's feathers
9. waistband (line)
10. pant cuffs (line)

Seasonal Activities • EMC 2004 • © Evan-Moor Corp.   Autumn   21

Page 22

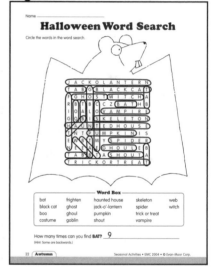

Halloween Word Search

Circle the words in the word search.

Word Box

bat	frighten	skeleton	web
black cat	ghost	spider	witch
boo	ghoul	jack-o'-lantern	trick or treat
costume	goblin	haunted house	vampire
		pumpkin	
		shout	

How many times can you find **BAT**?   9
(Hint: Some are backwards.)

22   Autumn   Seasonal Activities • EMC 2004 • © Evan-Moor Corp.

Page 23

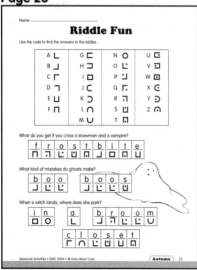

Riddle Fun

Use the code to find the answers to the riddles.

What do you get if you cross a snowman and a vampire?
f r o s t b i t e

What kind of mistakes do ghosts make?
b o o   b o o s

When a witch lands, where does she park?
i n   a   b r o o m
c l o s e t

Seasonal Activities • EMC 2004 • © Evan-Moor Corp.   Autumn   23

Page 24

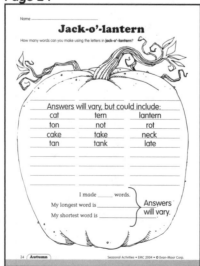

Jack-o'-lantern

How many words can you make using the letters in **jack-o'-lantern**?

Answers will vary, but could include:

cat	tern	lantern
ton	not	rot
cake	take	neck
tan	tank	late

I made ____ words.

My longest word is ____
My shortest word is ____

Answers will vary.

24   Autumn   Seasonal Activities • EMC 2004 • © Evan-Moor Corp.

Page 25

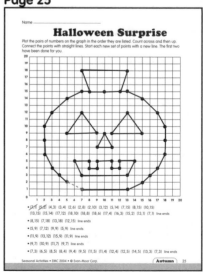

Halloween Surprise

Plot the pairs of numbers on the graph in the order they are listed. Count across and then up. Connect the points with straight lines. Start each new set of points with a new line. The first two have been done for you.

- (3,7) (3,9) (4,3) (3,4) (2,6) (2,10) (3,12) (5,14) (7,15) (8,15) (10,15) (13,15) (15,14) (17,12) (18,10) (18,8) (18,6) (17,4) (16,3) (13,2) (13,1) (7,1) line ends
- (8,15) (7,18) (13,18) (12,15) line ends
- (5,9) (7,12) (9,9) (5,9) line ends
- (11,9) (13,12) (15,9) (11,9) line ends
- (9,7) (10,9) (11,7) (9,7) line ends
- (7,3) (8,5) (8,4) (9,4) (9,5) (11,5) (11,4) (12,4) (12,5) (14,5) (13,3) (7,3) line ends

Seasonal Activities • EMC 2004 • © Evan-Moor Corp.   Autumn   25

Page 26

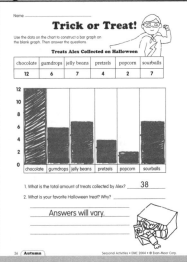

Name

Trick or Treat!

Use the data on the chart to construct a bar graph on the blank graph. Then answer the questions.

Treats Alex Collected on Halloween

chocolate	gumdrops	jelly beans	pretzels	popcorn	sourballs
12	6	7	4	2	7

(bar graph with values 12, 6, 7, 4, 2, 7 for chocolate, gumdrops, jelly beans, pretzels, popcorn, sourballs)

1. What is the total amount of treats collected by Alex? __38__

2. What is your favorite Halloween treat? Why?

__Answers will vary.__

Page 27

Name

Thanksgiving Day

Read the paragraph and then answer the questions.

Days of thanksgiving are celebrated all over the world. It is a day to give thanks for the blessings of the year.

In 1621, the Pilgrims had a feast to celebrate their first harvest in the New World. The feast lasted for three days. Governor Bradford of Plymouth Colony ordered this time for feasting and giving thanks.

The Thanksgiving Day we know became a national holiday in 1789. It is still a time to give thanks for our blessings. It is a time to celebrate with our friends and family.

1. What did the Pilgrims have to be thankful for in 1621?
__their first harvest__

2. When was Thanksgiving made a national holiday?
__1789__

Page 29

Note: Use this page after students have read the material on page 28.

The *Mayflower* Voyage

Fill in the blanks to complete the page.

The voyage began on __Sept. 6, 1620__.

There were __102__ passengers.

List three problems the passengers had aboard ship.
1. __too crowded__
2. __not enough food__
3. __stormy seas__

They landed at the tip of __Cape Cod__.

The voyage lasted __66__ days.

They reached land on __Nov. 11, 1620__.

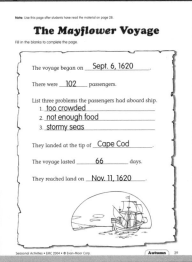

Page 30

Name

The *Mayflower*

Count by 2s to connect the dots.

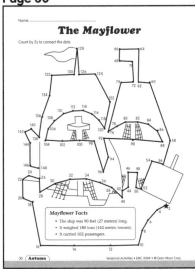

***Mayflower* Facts**
- The ship was 90 feet (27 meters) long.
- It weighed 180 tons (162 metric tonnes).
- It carried 102 passengers.

Page 31

Name

The First Year

Read about the Pilgrims and then answer the questions.

The Pilgrims chose land near a small bay as a place to live. They called their settlement Plymouth. They lived on board the ship until they could build homes. When weather permitted, many of the settlers went ashore and cut down timber to build temporary shelters.

In March, the weather improved. The settlers were able to start work on family gardens. They were able to build permanent houses. They planted seeds from England. These seeds did not grow well in the rocky soil. These early Pilgrims did not know how to hunt or fish, so food was running low. The arrival of two Native Americans brought the help the settlers needed.

Squanto, a Patuxet Indian, taught them how to hunt. He showed them how to plant native plants. Samoset, an Abnaki Indian, and Squanto reassured the local Wampanoag Indians that the Pilgrims were peaceful. The Pilgrims were thankful to the Indians for helping them survive their first year in the New World.

1. What problems did the settlers face?
__They could not grow food. They did not know how to hunt and fish.__

2. What type of help did Samoset and Squanto provide for the Pilgrims?
__They taught the Pilgrims how to hunt and plant native plants.__

Page 32

Name

A Peace Treaty

Read about the treaty and then answer the questions.

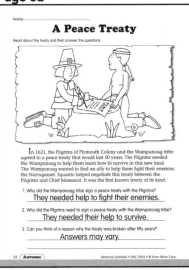

In 1621, the Pilgrims of Plymouth Colony and the Wampanoag tribe agreed to a peace treaty that would last 50 years. The Pilgrims needed the Wampanoag to help them learn how to survive in this new land. The Wampanoag wanted to find an ally to help them fight their enemies, the Narraganset. Squanto helped negotiate this treaty between the Pilgrims and Chief Massasoit. It was the first known treaty of its kind.

1. Why did the Pilgrims sign a peace treaty with the Pilgrims?
__They needed help to fight their enemies.__

2. Why did the Pilgrims need to sign a peace treaty with the Wampanoag tribe?
__They needed their help to survive.__

3. Can you think of a reason why the treaty was broken after fifty years?
__Answers may vary.__

Page 33

Name

Working in Plymouth Colony

While most people in Plymouth Colony were farmers, raising grains for cornmeal and flour, and raising cows, pigs, sheep, and chickens for food and wool, there were also craftspeople who made things for other people. For example, the farmer took his grain to the miller, who ground it into flour for the farmer.

- The **blacksmith** made things out of iron.
- The **cobbler** fixed shoes and boots.
- The **cooper** made wooden barrels.
- The **hatter** made plain and fancy hats.
- The **miller** ground the grains into flour.
- The **housewright** built houses.

Find the bolded words above as well as the words below in the word search.

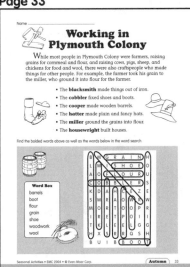

Word Box
barrels
boot
flour
grain
shoe
woodwork
wool

Page 35

Name

Thanksgiving Crossword Puzzle

Use the clues below to solve the crossword puzzle.

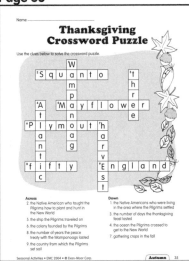

(Crossword answers: 2 across: Squanto; across: Mayflower; Plymouth; fifty; England; down: Wampanoag)

Across
2. the Native American who taught the Pilgrims how to plant and hunt in the New World
5. the ship the Pilgrims traveled on
6. the colony founded by the Pilgrims
8. the number of years the peace treaty with the Wampanoags lasted
9. the country from which the Pilgrims set sail

Down
1. the Native Americans who were living in the area where the Pilgrims settled
3. the number of days the thanksgiving feast lasted
4. the ocean the Pilgrims crossed to get to the New World
7. gathering crops in the fall

Page 36

Name

New World Food Plants

Circle the foods that came from the New World.

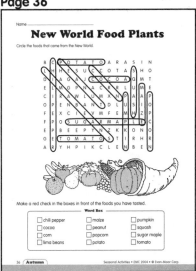

Make a red check in the boxes in front of the foods you have tasted.

Word Box

☐ chili pepper	☐ maize	☐ pumpkin
☐ cocoa	☐ peanut	☐ squash
☐ corn	☐ popcorn	☐ sugar maple
☐ lima beans	☐ potato	☐ tomato

Page 37

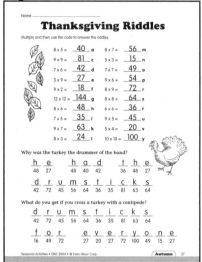

Thanksgiving Riddles

Multiply and then use the code to answer the riddles.

8 x 5 =	**40** o	8 x 7 =	**56** m
9 x 9 =	**81** c	5 x 3 =	**15** n
7 x 6 =	**42** d	7 x 7 =	**49** o
3 x 9 =	**27** e	9 x 6 =	**54** p
9 x 2 =	**18** f	8 x 9 =	**72** r
12 x 12 =	**144** g	8 x 8 =	**64** s
8 x 6 =	**48** h	6 x 6 =	**36** t
7 x 5 =	**35** i	9 x 5 =	**45** u
9 x 7 =	**63** k	5 x 4 =	**20** v
8 x 3 =	**24** l	10 x 10 =	**100** y

Why was the turkey the drummer of the band?

h e   h a d   t h e
48 27   27 40 42   36 48 27

d r u m s t i c k s
42 72 45 56 64 36 35 81 63 64

What do you get if you cross a turkey with a centipede?

d r u m s t i c k s
42 72 45 56 64 36 35 81 63 64

f o r   e v e r y o n e
16 49 72   27 20 27 72 100 49 15 27

Seasonal Activities • EMC 2004 • © Evan-Moor Corp.   Autumn   37

Page 40

Let's Eat!

Unscramble the words to find what foods were served at the first thanksgiving feast.

kinpumsp	**pumpkins**	soeog	**goose**
nipturs	**turnips**	macls	**clams**
nroc	**corn**	soyters	**oysters**
ered	**deer**	bagcabe	**cabbage**
keytur	**turkey**	lee	**eel**
cudk	**duck**	soblter	**lobster**

Word Box

cabbage	deer	goose	pumpkins
clams	duck	lobster	turkey
corn	eel	oysters	turnips

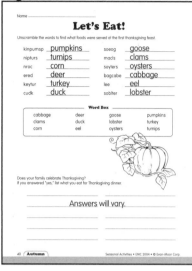

Does your family celebrate Thanksgiving?
If you answered "yes," list what you eat for Thanksgiving dinner.

Answers will vary.

40   Autumn   Seasonal Activities • EMC 2004 • © Evan-Moor Corp.

Page 43

Snow Words

Write the word for each definition. All answers contain the word **snow**.
Then write the circled letters in order on these lines.

s n o w m a n
1 2 3 4 5 6

1. small white flakes falling from the sky
s n o w f l a k e (s)

2. a small round mass of snow packed together
s (n) o w b a l l

3. a warm garment worn by children in very cold weather
s n o (w) s u i t

4. a device used to push or throw snow off a road
s n o w p l o (w)

5. a motor vehicle used to travel over snow
s n o w m (o) b i l e

6. a heap of snow blown together by the wind
s n o w b (a) n k

7. wooden and leather frames worn on feet when walking on snow
s (n) o w s h o e s

Draw the mystery object on the back of this page.

Seasonal Activities • EMC 2004 • © Evan-Moor Corp.   Winter   43

Page 44

Winter Word Search

Find these winter words and circle them.

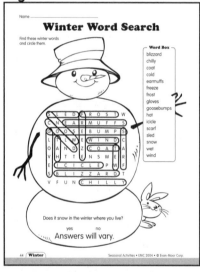

Word Box

blizzard
chilly
coat
cold
earmuffs
freeze
frost
gloves
goosebumps
hat
icicle
scarf
sled
snow
wet
wind

Does it snow in the winter where you live?

yes   no
Answers will vary.

44   Winter   Seasonal Activities • EMC 2004 • © Evan-Moor Corp.

Page 46

What's for Breakfast?

Count by 12s and then use the code to answer the riddle.

A	**12**	K	**60**	R	**96**
D	**24**	L	**72**	S	**108**
E	**36**	O	**84**	T	**120**
F	**48**				

What do snowmen eat for breakfast?

f r o s t e d
48 96 84 108 120 36 24

f l a k e s
48 72 12 60 36 108

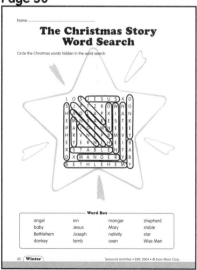

What do you like to eat for breakfast on a cold day?

Answers will vary.

46   Winter   Seasonal Activities • EMC 2004 • © Evan-Moor Corp.

Page 47

Bill of Rights Day

Read about the Bill of Rights and then answer the questions.

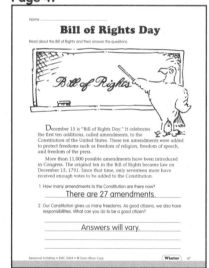

Bill of Rights

December 15 is "Bill of Rights Day." It celebrates the first ten additions, called amendments, to the Constitution of the United States. These ten amendments were added to protect freedoms such as freedom of religion, freedom of speech, and freedom of the press.

More than 11,000 possible amendments have been introduced in Congress. The original ten in the Bill of Rights became law on December 15, 1791. Since that time, only seventeen more have received enough votes to be added to the Constitution.

1. How many amendments to the Constitution are there now?
There are 27 amendments.

2. Our Constitution gives us many freedoms. As good citizens, we also have responsibilities. What can you do to be a good citizen?

Answers will vary.

Seasonal Activities • EMC 2004 • © Evan-Moor Corp.   Winter   47

Page 49

Christmas

Read about Christmas and then answer the questions.

Christmas is a celebration of the birth of Jesus. On December 25, Christians around the world celebrate His birth with church services, the giving of gifts, the singing of carols, and family gatherings.

1. Who celebrates Christmas?
Christians

2. How is the holiday celebrated?
giving gifts, singing carols, family gatherings

3. Does your family celebrate Christmas?   Answers will vary.
If yes, how do you celebrate?
Answers will vary.

44   Winter   Seasonal Activities • EMC 2004 • © Evan-Moor Corp.   49

Page 50

The Christmas Story Word Search

Circle the Christmas words hidden in the word search.

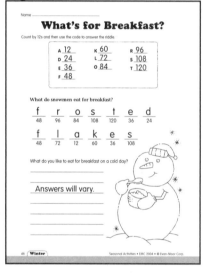

Word Box

angel	inn	manger	shepherd
baby	Jesus	Mary	stable
Bethlehem	Joseph	nativity	star
donkey	lamb	oxen	Wise Men

50   Winter   Seasonal Activities • EMC 2004 • © Evan-Moor Corp.

Page 51

We Three Kings

Help the Three Kings reach Bethlehem.

The Three Kings brought gifts to the baby Jesus.
What gift would you take to the new baby?

Answers will vary.

Seasonal Activities • EMC 2004 • © Evan-Moor Corp.   Winter   51

Page 52

Las Posadas

Count by 3s to connect the dots. Read the story and then answer the questions.

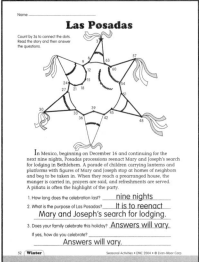

In Mexico, beginning on December 16 and continuing for the next nine nights, Posadas processions reenact Mary and Joseph's search for lodging in Bethlehem. A parade of children carrying lanterns and platforms with figures of Mary and Joseph stop at homes of neighbors and beg to be taken in. When they reach a prearranged house, the manger is carried in, prayers are said, and refreshments are served. A piñata is often the highlight of the party.

1. How long does the celebration last? __nine nights__
2. What is the purpose of Las Posadas? __It is to reenact Mary and Joseph's search for lodging.__
3. Does your family celebrate this holiday? __Answers will vary.__
   If yes, how do you celebrate? __Answers will vary.__

Page 53

Merry Christmas Crossword Puzzle

Use the clues to solve the crossword puzzle.

Across
1. a reindeer with a shiny red nose
3. an evergreen tree
4. a plant with prickly leaves and red berries
5. white lacy flakes that fall from the sky
6. decorations for a Christmas tree
9. the night before a holiday
11. another word for "present"

Down
1. eight of these pull Santa's sleigh
2. a special day for celebration
3. some children hang this above the fireplace on Christmas Eve
7. a vehicle for traveling over snow
8. a chubby man who is supposed to bring presents to good children
10. a worker in Santa's workshop

Page 54

Take a Close Look

Find 10 differences between the two pictures.

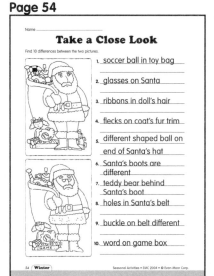

1. soccer ball in toy bag
2. glasses on Santa
3. ribbons in doll's hair
4. flecks on coat's fur trim
5. different shaped ball on end of Santa's hat
6. Santa's boots are different
7. teddy bear behind Santa's boot
8. holes in Santa's belt
9. buckle on belt different
10. word on game box

Page 55

Name That Christmas Tune!

Use the code to name some favorite old Christmas songs.

1. Deck the Halls
2. We Three Kings
3. Away in a Manger
4. Jingle Bells

Write the name of your favorite Christmas song in code.
__Answers will vary.__

Page 56

Celebrate Hanukkah

Read about Hanukkah and then answer the questions.

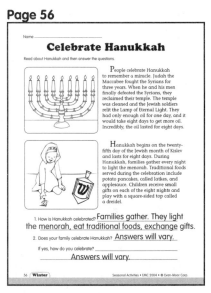

People celebrate Hanukkah to remember a miracle. Judah the Maccabee fought the Syrians for three years. When he and his men finally defeated the Syrians, they reclaimed their temple. The temple was cleaned and the Jewish soldiers relit the Lamp of Eternal Light. They had only enough oil for one day, and it would take eight days to get more oil. Incredibly, the oil lasted for eight days.

Hanukkah begins on the twenty-fifth day of the Jewish month of Kislev and lasts for eight days. During Hanukkah, families gather every night to light the menorah. Traditional foods served during the celebration include potato pancakes, called latkes, and applesauce. Children receive small gifts on each of the eight nights and play with a square-sided top called a dreidel.

1. How is Hanukkah celebrated? __Families gather. They light the menorah, eat traditional foods, exchange gifts.__
2. Does your family celebrate Hanukkah? __Answers will vary.__
   If yes, how do you celebrate? __Answers will vary.__

Page 57

The Dreidel Game

Read about the dreidel game and then answer the question.

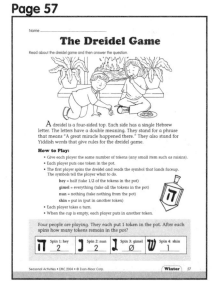

A dreidel is a four-sided top. Each side has a single Hebrew letter. The letters have a double meaning. They stand for a phrase that means "A great miracle happened here." They also stand for Yiddish words that give rules for the dreidel game.

How to Play:
- Give each player the same number of tokens (any small item such as raisins).
- Each player puts one token in the pot.
- The first player spins the dreidel and reads the symbol that lands faceup. The symbols tell the player what to do.
  - hey = half (take 1/2 of the tokens in the pot)
  - gimel = everything (take all the tokens in the pot)
  - nun = nothing (take nothing from the pot)
  - shin = put in (put in another token)
- Each player takes a turn.
- When the cup is empty, each player puts in another token.

Four people are playing. They each put 1 token in the pot. After each spins how many tokens remain in the pot?

Spin 1: hey	Spin 2: nun	Spin 3: gimel	Spin 4: shin
2	2	0	1

Page 58

About Kwanzaa

Read about Kwanzaa and then answer the questions.

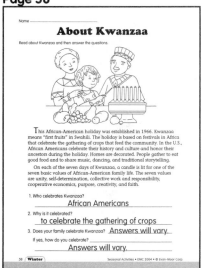

This African-American holiday was established in 1966. Kwanzaa means "first fruits" in Swahili. The holiday is based on festivals in Africa that celebrate the gathering of crops that feed the community. In the U.S., African Americans celebrate their history and culture and honor their ancestors during the holiday. Homes are decorated. People gather to eat good food and to share music, dancing, and traditional storytelling.

On each of the seven days of Kwanzaa, a candle is lit for one of the seven basic values of African-American family life. The seven values are unity, self-determination, collective work and responsibility, cooperative economics, purpose, creativity, and faith.

1. Who celebrates Kwanzaa? __African Americans__
2. Why is it celebrated? __to celebrate the gathering of crops__
3. Does your family celebrate Kwanzaa? __Answers will vary.__
   If yes, how do you celebrate? __Answers will vary.__

Page 59

Light the Kinara

Follow the steps at the bottom of the page to color the candles.

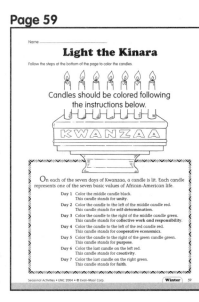

Candles should be colored following the instructions below.

On each of the seven days of Kwanzaa, a candle is lit. Each candle represents one of the seven basic values of African-American life.

Day 1 Color the middle candle black. This candle stands for **unity**.
Day 2 Color the candle to the left of the middle candle red. This candle stands for **self-determination**.
Day 3 Color the candle to the right of the middle candle green. This candle stands for **collective work and responsibility**.
Day 4 Color the candle to the left of the red candle red. This candle stands for **cooperative economics**.
Day 5 Color the candle to the right of the green candle green. This candle stands for **purpose**.
Day 6 Color the last candle on the left red. This candle stands for **creativity**.
Day 7 Color the last candle on the right green. This candle stands for **faith**.

Page 60

Happy 20___!

Read about New Year's and answer the questions. Then draw yourself in the celebration.

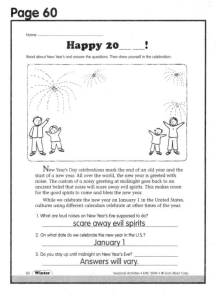

New Year's Day celebrations mark the end of an old year and the start of a new year. All over the world, the new year is greeted with noise. The custom of a noisy greeting at midnight goes back to an ancient belief that noise will scare away evil spirits. This makes room for the good spirits to come and bless the new year.

While we celebrate the new year on January 1 in the United States, cultures using different calendars celebrate at other times of the year.

1. What are loud noises on New Year's Eve supposed to do? __scare away evil spirits__
2. On what date do we celebrate the new year in the U.S.? __January 1__
3. Do you stay up until midnight on New Year's Eve? __Answers will vary.__

Page 61

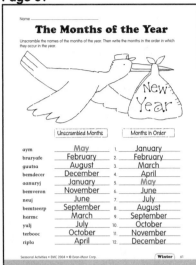

The Months of the Year

Unscramble the names of the months of the year. Then write the months in the order in which they occur in the year.

Unscrambled Months		Months in Order	
aym	May	1.	January
bruryafe	February	2.	February
guutsa	August	3.	March
bemdecer	December	4.	April
aanuryj	January	5.	May
bemveron	November	6.	June
neuj	June	7.	July
bemtseerp	September	8.	August
harmc	March	9.	September
yulj	July	10.	October
terbooc	October	11.	November
ripla	April	12.	December

Seasonal Activities • EMC 2004 • © Evan-Moor Corp. — Winter 61

Page 63

Dr. Martin Luther King, Jr.
A Modern Hero

Read about Dr. King and then answer the questions.

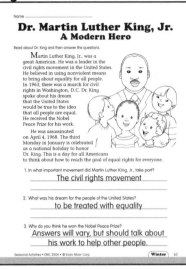

Martin Luther King, Jr., was a great American. He was a leader in the civil rights movement in the United States. He believed in using nonviolent means to bring about equality for all people. In 1963, there was a march for civil rights in Washington, D.C. Dr. King spoke about his dream that the United States would be true to the idea that all people are equal. He received the Nobel Peace Prize for his work.

He was assassinated on April 4, 1968. The third Monday in January is celebrated as a national holiday to honor Dr. King. This is a day for all Americans to think about how to reach the goal of equal rights for everyone.

1. In what important movement did Martin Luther King, Jr., take part?
   The civil rights movement

2. What was his dream for the people of the United States?
   to be treated with equality

3. Why do you think he won the Nobel Peace Prize?
   Answers will vary, but should talk about his work to help other people.

Seasonal Activities • EMC 2004 • © Evan-Moor Corp. — Winter 63

Page 64

Martin Luther King, Jr.
Crossword Puzzle

Use the clues to complete the crossword puzzle.

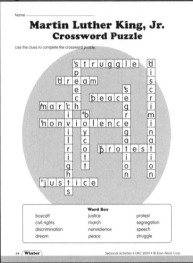

Word Box

boycott	justice	protest
civil rights	march	segregation
discrimination	nonviolence	speech
dream	peace	struggle

64 Winter — Seasonal Activities • EMC 2004 • © Evan-Moor Corp.

Page 67

Who Am I?

Use division to help you find my name.

Some people say I forecast the weather. Look out if I see my shadow!

A - 2	
E - 3	
H - 4	
I - 5	
L - 6	
N - 7	
P - 8	
S - 9	
T - 10	
U - 11	
W - 12	
X - 13	
Y - 14	

p 72 ÷ 9 = 8
u 99 ÷ 9 = 11
n 56 ÷ 8 = 7
x 182 ÷ 14 = 13
s 81 ÷ 9 = 9
u 275 ÷ 25 = 11
t 100 ÷ 10 = 10
a 100 ÷ 50 = 2
w 144 ÷ 12 = 12
n 140 ÷ 20 = 7
e 99 ÷ 33 = 3
y 42 ÷ 3 = 14

p 88 ÷ 11 = 8
h 36 ÷ 9 = 4
i 80 ÷ 16 = 5
l 72 ÷ 12 = 6

Color the picture that shows what kind of animal I am.

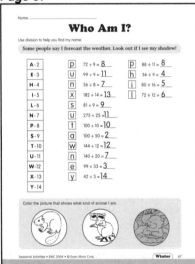

Seasonal Activities • EMC 2004 • © Evan-Moor Corp. — Winter 67

Page 68

Weather Watch

Punxsutawney Phil is a nervous groundhog. What will happen when he peeks out of his burrow? Will he see his shadow? Will it be raining? What will the weather be? Find the words below that describe weather. Write them in the box.

balmy	hazy
breezy	overcast
bright	pleasant
brisk	rainy
cloudy	stormy
foggy	sunshiny
foul	windy
gusty	

afraid	bright	excited	hazy	rainy	terrified
alarmed	brisk	foggy	jumpy	shy	uneasy
angry	cautious	foul	nervous	skittish	upset
balmy	cloudy	frightened	overcast	stormy	windy
breezy	happy	gusty	pleasant	sunshiny	

What do the remaining words describe? feelings

68 Winter — Seasonal Activities • EMC 2004 • © Evan-Moor Corp.

Page 69

Chinese New Year

Read about Chinese New Year and then answer the questions.
Count by 2s to connect the dots.

"Gung Hay Fat Choy!" Chinese New Year occurs on the first day of the first new moon after January 21. To get ready for the new year, families clean their houses from top to bottom. They wear new clothing. Good luck wishes are hung from windows. Children receive little red packets with coins inside.

The celebration includes a parade led by a long dragon, the symbol of good luck. People hold up the dragon and make it dance and weave through the streets. The dragon dance is believed to chase away bad luck. Firecrackers explode as the dragon passes.

1. Why doesn't Chinese New Year occur on the same day every year?
   It's based on the cycles of the moon.

2. How would you greet someone on Chinese New Year?
   "Gung Hay Fat Choy!"

Seasonal Activities • EMC 2004 • © Evan-Moor Corp. — Winter 69

Page 70

Note: Reproduce page 71 to use with this page.

Tangrams

It is believed that the tangram puzzle originated in China about 250 years ago.

Use your tangram pieces to make this rooster in the box.

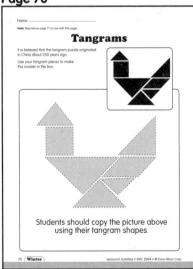

Students should copy the picture above using their tangram shapes.

70 Winter — Seasonal Activities • EMC 2004 • © Evan-Moor Corp.

Page 73

Presidents' Day

Read about Presidents' Day and then answer the questions.

The birthdays of Abraham Lincoln (February 12) and George Washington (February 22) were once celebrated as separate holidays. Since 1971, both presidents have been honored on the same day, the third Monday in February. Presidents' Day is a day to honor all of America's past presidents.

1. Before 1971, when were Lincoln's and Washington's birthdays celebrated?
   Lincoln on Feb.12 and Washington on Feb. 22

2. Why do you think we celebrate Presidents' Day instead of Washington's birthday and Lincoln's birthday? So we can honor all the past presidents.

Seasonal Activities • EMC 2004 • © Evan-Moor Corp. — Winter 73

Page 74

George Washington

Draw President Washington's face by following the grid. Then read about Washington's life.

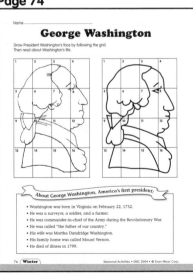

About George Washington, America's first president.

- Washington was born in Virginia on February 22, 1732.
- He was a surveyor, a soldier, and a farmer.
- He was commander-in-chief of the Army during the Revolutionary War.
- He was called "the father of our country."
- His wife was Martha Dandridge Washington.
- His family home was called Mount Vernon.
- He died of illness in 1799.

74 Winter — Seasonal Activities • EMC 2004 • © Evan-Moor Corp.

Page 75

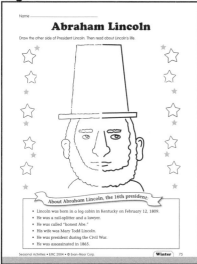

Abraham Lincoln

Draw the other side of President Lincoln. Then read about Lincoln's life.

About Abraham Lincoln, the 16th president.

- Lincoln was born in a log cabin in Kentucky on February 12, 1809.
- He was a rail-splitter and a lawyer.
- He was called "honest Abe."
- His wife was Mary Todd Lincoln.
- He was president during the Civil War.
- He was assassinated in 1865.

Seasonal Activities • EMC 2004 • © Evan-Moor Corp.   Winter   75

Page 76

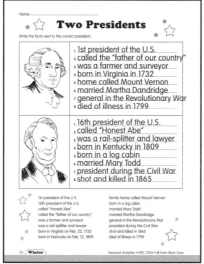

Two Presidents

Write the facts next to the correct president.

1. 1st president of the U.S.
2. called the "father of our country"
3. was a farmer and surveyor
4. born in Virginia in 1732
5. home called Mount Vernon
6. married Martha Dandridge
7. general in the Revolutionary War
8. died of illness in 1799

1. 16th president of the U.S.
2. called "Honest Abe"
3. was a rail-splitter and lawyer
4. born in Kentucky in 1809
5. born in a log cabin
6. married Mary Todd
7. president during the Civil War
8. shot and killed in 1865

1st president of the U.S.
16th president of the U.S.
called "Honest Abe"
called the "father of our country"
was a farmer and surveyor
was a rail-splitter and lawyer
born in Virginia in Feb. 22, 1732
born in Kentucky on Feb. 12, 1809

family home called Mount Vernon
born in a log cabin
married Mary Todd
married Martha Dandridge
general in the Revolutionary War
president during the Civil War
shot and killed in 1865
died of illness in 1799

76   Winter   Seasonal Activities • EMC 2004 • © Evan-Moor Corp.

Page 77

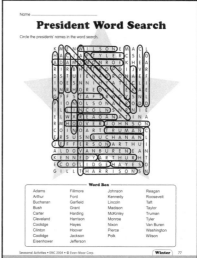

President Word Search

Circle the presidents' names in the word search.

Word Box

Adams	Fillmore	Johnson	Reagan
Arthur	Ford	Kennedy	Roosevelt
Buchanan	Garfield	Lincoln	Taft
Bush	Grant	Madison	Taylor
Carter	Harding	McKinley	Truman
Cleveland	Harrison	Monroe	Tyler
Coolidge	Hayes	Nixon	Van Buren
Clinton	Hoover	Pierce	Washington
Coolidge	Jackson	Polk	Wilson
Eisenhower	Jefferson		

Seasonal Activities • EMC 2004 • © Evan-Moor Corp.   Winter   77

Page 79

Valentine Messages

Use the code to solve the riddles.

A = 26	G = 20	L = 15	Q = 10	V = 5
B = 25	H = 19	M = 14	R = 9	W = 4
C = 24	I = 18	N = 13	S = 8	X = 3
D = 23	J = 17	O = 12	T = 7	Y = 2
E = 22	K = 16	P = 11	U = 6	Z = 1
F = 21				

What did the pig write to his sweetheart?
h o g s   a n d   k i s s e s
19 12 20 8 26 13 23 16 18 8 8 22 8

What did the owl write to her sweetheart?
o w l   a l w a y s   b e
12 4 15 26 15 4 26 2 8 25 22
y o u r   v a l e n t i n e
2 12 6 9 5 26 15 22 13 7 18 13 22

What did the bee say to his sweetheart?
y o u' r e   a   h o n e y
2 12 6 9 22 26 19 12 13 22 2
o f   a   v a l e n t i n e
12 21 26 5 26 15 22 13 7 18 13 22

What would you write to your sweetheart? Write the message in code.
Answers will vary.

Seasonal Activities • EMC 2004 • © Evan-Moor Corp.   Winter   79

Page 80

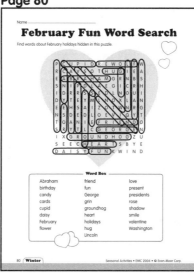

February Fun Word Search

Find words about February holidays hidden in this puzzle.

Word Box

Abraham	friend	love
birthday	fun	present
candy	George	presidents
cards	grin	rose
cupid	groundhog	shadow
daisy	heart	smile
February	holidays	valentine
flower	hug	Washington
	Lincoln	

80   Winter   Seasonal Activities • EMC 2004 • © Evan-Moor Corp.

Page 81

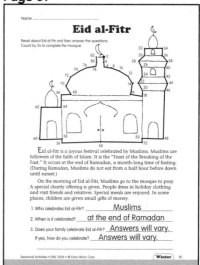

Eid al-Fitr

Read about Eid al-Fitr and then answer the questions.
Count by 2s to complete the mosque.

Eid al-Fitr is a joyous festival celebrated by Muslims. Muslims are followers of the faith of Islam. It is the "Feast of the Breaking of the Fast." It occurs at the end of Ramadan, a month-long time of fasting. (During Ramadan, Muslims do not eat from a half hour before dawn until sunset.)

On the morning of Eid al-Fitr, Muslims go to the mosque to pray. A special charity offering is given. People dress in holiday clothing and visit friends and relatives. Special meals are enjoyed. In some places, children are given small gifts of money.

1. Who celebrates Eid al-Fitr?   Muslims
2. When is it celebrated?   at the end of Ramadan
3. Does your family celebrate Eid al-Fitr?   Answers will vary.
   If yes, how do you celebrate?   Answers will vary.

Seasonal Activities • EMC 2004 • © Evan-Moor Corp.   Winter   81

Page 82

Tet Nguyen Dan

Read about Tet and then answer the questions.

The Vietnamese celebration Tet Nguyen Dan begins on the first day of the first month of the lunar new year. It is the largest celebration of the year. It is like New Year's, Thanksgiving, Fourth of July, and a birthday party for everyone all in one holiday. The holiday lasts three days.

The house is cleaned, food is prepared, and new clothes are bought. Family members return home to visit. Gifts are given at Tet. Children receive money in red envelopes. People enjoy fireworks, sporting events, concerts, dragon dancing, and singing.

1. How do the Vietnamese get ready for Tet? They clean their homes, prepare food, and buy new clothes.
2. Describe one way Tet is celebrated: Gifts are given, children get money, they have fireworks, etc.
3. Does your family celebrate Tet?   Answers will vary.
   If yes, how do you celebrate?   Answers will vary.

82   Winter   Seasonal Activities • EMC 2004 • © Evan-Moor Corp.

Page 85

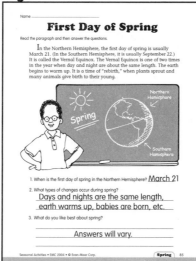

First Day of Spring

Read the paragraph and then answer the questions.

In the Northern Hemisphere, the first day of spring is usually March 21. (In the Southern Hemisphere, it is usually September 22.) It is called the Vernal Equinox. The Vernal Equinox is one of two times in the year when day and night are about the same length. The earth begins to warm up. It is a time of "rebirth," when plants sprout and many animals give birth to their young.

1. When is the first day of spring in the Northern Hemisphere? March 21
2. What types of changes occur during spring?
   Days and nights are the same length, earth warms up, babies are born, etc.
3. What do you like best about spring?
   Answers will vary.

Seasonal Activities • EMC 2004 • © Evan-Moor Corp.   Spring   85

Page 86

March Winds

Complete the crossword puzzle with "wind" words.

Across
1. a ship with sails
3. a machine that generates power using the wind
4. moving air
5. an unexpected lucky event or unexpected money

Down
1. the tube connecting the throat and lungs, the trachea
2. a person who says nothing interesting or important
3. a sheet of glass in front of the driver and riders in a vehicle

Word Box
wind
windbag
windfall
windjammer
windmill
windpipe
windshield

86   Spring   Seasonal Activities • EMC 2004 • © Evan-Moor Corp.

Page 87

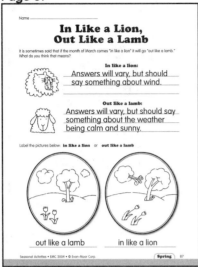

In Like a Lion, Out Like a Lamb

It is sometimes said that if the month of March comes "in like a lion" it will go "out like a lamb." What do you think that means?

In like a lion:
Answers will vary, but should say something about wind.

Out like a lamb:
Answers will vary, but should say something about the weather being calm and sunny.

Label the pictures below: **in like a lion** or **out like a lamb**

out like a lamb   in like a lion

Page 88

April Showers

Count by 3s. Then use the code to answer the riddle about rainy April days.

a	3	i	21	r	39
b	6	k	24	s	42
c	9	l	27	t	45
d	12	n	30	u	48
e	15	o	33	v	51
h	18	p	36	w	54

Why don't mother kangaroos like April showers?

b e c a u s e   t h e
6 15 9 3 48 42 15   45 18 15

k i d s   h a v e   t o
24 21 12 42   18 3 51 15   45 33

p l a y   i n d o o r s
36 27 3 54   21 30 12 33 33 39 42

Page 89

March Winds and April Showers

Find the hidden weather words.

Word Box

breeze	heat	mist	raindrops	temperature
cloudy	high	moisture	showers	thunder
dew	lightning	precipitation	storm	weather
drips	low	rain	sunshine	wind
fog				

Page 90

May Flowers

Write the flower names in alphabetical order.

buttercup	petunia	azalea
daffodil	orchid	carnation
honeysuckle	nasturtium	larkspur
violet	aster	zinnia
snapdragon	crocus	jasmine
marigold	daisy	begonia
hollyhock	lily	iris
rose	tulip	sweet pea

1. aster
2. azalea
3. begonia
4. buttercup
5. carnation
6. crocus
7. daffodil
8. daisy
9. hollyhock
10. honeysuckle
11. iris
12. jasmine
13. larkspur
14. lily
15. marigold
16. nasturtium
17. orchid
18. petunia
19. rose
20. snapdragon
21. sweet pea
22. tulip
23. violet
24. zinnia

List your four favorite flowers here.
1. Answers will vary.
2.
3.
4.

Page 91

Johnny Appleseed

Read about Johnny Appleseed and then answer the question.

John Chapman was a tree farmer. In the 1800s, he set out to explore the Northwest Territory. As he wandered, he carried a bag of apple seeds on his back. When he found a good spot, he would clear the land and plant apple trees. People began to call him "Johnny Appleseed."

As time went by, he became a folk hero. Many things people say he did were probably imaginary. But we do know that he planted a large number of apple trees on the early frontier.

How did John Chapman earn his nickname?
He planted lots of apple trees, so they called him Johnny Appleseed.

Page 92

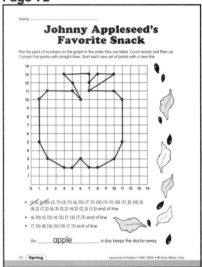

Johnny Appleseed's Favorite Snack

Plot the pairs of numbers on the graph in the order they are listed. Count across and then up. Connect the points with straight lines. Start each new set of points with a new line.

• (1,5) (1,10) (2,11) (5,11) (6,10) (7,11) (10,11) (11,10) (11,5) (10,3) (8,2) (7,2) (6,3) (5,2) (4,2) (2,3) (1,5) end of line
• (6,10) (5,12) (4,13) (7,13) (7,11) end of line
• (7,12) (8,13) (10,13) (7,11) end of line

An apple a day keeps the doctor away.

Page 93

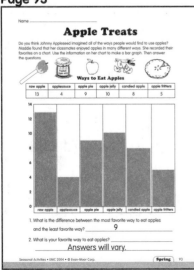

Apple Treats

Do you think Johnny Appleseed imagined all of the ways people would find to use apples? Maddie found that her classmates enjoyed apples in many different ways. She recorded their favorites on a chart. Use the information on her chart to make a bar graph. Then answer the questions.

Ways to Eat Apples

raw apple	applesauce	apple pie	apple jelly	candied apple	apple fritters
13	4	9	10	8	5

1. What is the difference between the most favorite way to eat apples and the least favorite way? 9
2. What is your favorite way to eat apples?
   Answers will vary.

Page 94

The Tree Planter

Draw a line to guide Johnny Appleseed through the woods to the cabin.

Page 95

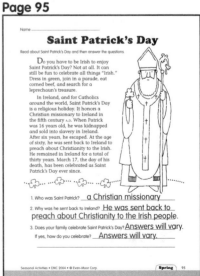

Saint Patrick's Day

Read about Saint Patrick's Day and then answer the questions.

Do you have to be Irish to enjoy Saint Patrick's Day? Not at all. It can still be fun to celebrate all things "Irish." Dress in green, join in a parade, eat corned beef, and search for a leprechaun's treasure.

In Ireland, and for Catholics around the world, Saint Patrick's Day is a religious holiday. It honors a Christian missionary to Ireland in the fifth century A.D. When Patrick was 16 years old, he was kidnapped and sold into slavery in Ireland. After six years, he escaped. At the age of sixty, he was sent back to Ireland to preach about Christianity to the Irish. He remained in Ireland for a total of thirty years. March 17, the day of his death, has been celebrated as Saint Patrick's Day ever since.

1. Who was Saint Patrick? a Christian missionary
2. Why was he sent back to Ireland? He was sent back to preach about Christianity to the Irish people
3. Does your family celebrate Saint Patrick's Day? Answers will vary.
   If yes, how do you celebrate? Answers will vary.

Leprechauns

Read about leprechauns and then answer the question.
Draw the other side of the leprechaun.

A leprechaun is a type of Irish fairy. Leprechauns are said to be mean and spiteful. They are also said to be rich. Look carefully under mushrooms or in fields of clover, and you might catch one. If you do, he might offer you his pot of gold if you'll release him. Keep a close eye on the leprechaun, or he will vanish without paying you!

Give three reasons why you know leprechauns are not real!
1. They are a type of fairy.
2. They live under mushrooms and clover.
3. They have pots of gold.

A Pot of Gold

Find 10 differences between these leprechauns.

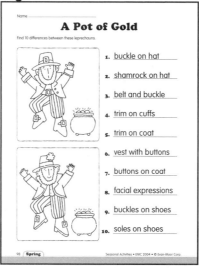

1. buckle on hat
2. shamrock on hat
3. belt and buckle
4. trim on cuffs
5. trim on coat
6. vest with buttons
7. buttons on coat
8. facial expressions
9. buckles on shoes
10. soles on shoes

Saint Patrick's Day Word Search

Find the words hidden in the puzzle.

Word Box

blarney	Ireland	rainbow
cabbage	Irish	Saint Patrick
capture	lad	shamrock
catch	lass	shillelagh
Emerald Isle	leprechaun	silver
Erin	luck	tiny
gold	magic	toadstool
green	March	treasure
hide	mushroom	wee
hunt	potato	wishes

What Is It?

Use the code to find the answers.

A ⌐	G ⌐	N ○	U ⌐
B ⌐	H ⌐	O ⌐	V ⌐
C ⌐	I ⌐	P ⌐	W ⌐
D ⌐	J ⌐	Q ⌐	X ⌐
E ⌐	K ⌐	R ⌐	Y ⌐
F ⌐	L ⌐	S ⌐	Z ⌐
	M ⌐	T ⌐	

a tricky Irish elf
l e p r e c h a u n

"lucky" green leaves
s h a m r o c k s

vegetables with "eyes"
p o t a t o e s

a nickname for Ireland
E m e r a l d   I s l e

a kind of Irish talk that flatters you
b l a r n e y

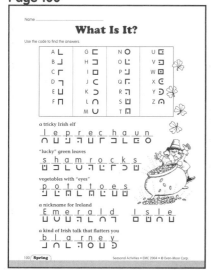

Earth Day Word Search

Find the words hidden in the puzzle.

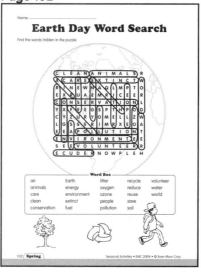

Word Box

air	Earth	litter	volunteer
animals	energy	oxygen	water
care	environment	ozone	world
clean	extinct	people	
conservation	fuel	pollution	soil
		recycle	
		reduce	
		reuse	
		save	

Arbor Day

Read about Arbor Day and then complete the word search.

Arbor Day was started in 1872. It is a day to honor and plant trees. On April 10, 1872, Arbor Day was first celebrated in Nebraska with the planting of over one million trees. Arbor Day is celebrated in different states on different days, but it is usually near April 22.

Trees provide us with many useful products. See how many you can find in the word search.

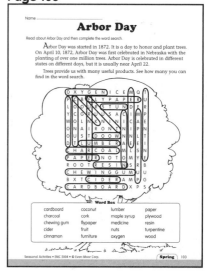

Word Box

cardboard	coconut	lumber	paper
charcoal	cork	maple syrup	plywood
chewing gum	flypaper	medicine	resin
cider	fruit	nuts	turpentine
cinnamon	furniture	oxygen	wood

Arbor Day Crossword Puzzle

Use the clues to complete the crossword puzzle.

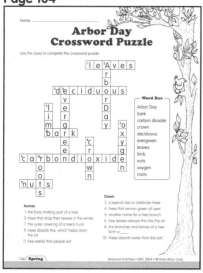

Word Box
Arbor Day
bark
carbon dioxide
crown
deciduous
evergreen
leaves
limb
nuts
oxygen
roots

Across
1. the food-making part of a tree
3. trees that drop their leaves in the winter
7. the outer covering of a tree's trunk
9. trees absorb this, which helps clean the air
11. tree seeds that people eat

Down
2. a special day to celebrate trees
4. trees that remain green all year
5. a tree branch
6. tree leaves release this into the air
8. the branches and leaves of a tree form a ___
10. these absorb water from the soil

Tree Alphabet

Write the tree names in alphabetical order.

beech	ginko	eucalyptus	holly	pine
apple	yew	oak	quince	maple
fir	laurel	fig	locust	walnut
willow	dogwood	juniper	redbud	orange
cedar	spruce	palm	sycamore	birch
elm				

1. apple
2. beech
3. birch
4. cedar
5. dogwood
6. elm
7. eucalyptus
8. fig
9. fir
10. ginko
11. holly
12. juniper
13. laurel
14. locust
15. maple
16. oak
17. orange
18. palm
19. pine
20. quince
21. redbud
22. spruce
23. sycamore
24. walnut
25. willow
26. yew

Circle the letters that are not used in your tree alphabet.

a b c d e f g h (i) (j) (k) l m (n)
o p q r s (t) (u) (v) (x) y (z)

Easter

Read about Easter and then answer the questions.
Draw a line to lead the family to church on Easter Sunday.

Easter is one of the most important religious holidays of the year for Christians. It is a time of joy, with special church services and festive meals.

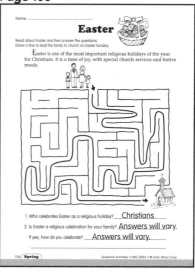

1. Who celebrates Easter as a religious holiday? Christians
2. Is Easter a religious celebration for your family? Answers will vary.
   If yes, how do you celebrate? Answers will vary.

Page 107

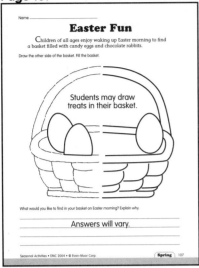

Easter Fun

Children of all ages enjoy waking up Easter morning to find a basket filled with candy eggs and chocolate rabbits.

Draw the other side of the basket. Fill the basket.

Students may draw treats in their basket.

What would you like to find in your basket on Easter morning? Explain why.

Answers will vary.

Page 108

Pysanky Eggs

Ukrainian Easter eggs are decorated with symbols of good wishes. These beautiful eggs are then given to special friends and family members. Here are some of the symbols used and what they mean:

- flower—love
- pine tree—love
- reindeer—wealth
- spiral—growing
- hen and rooster—wishes coming true

Decorate this egg with an "Easter wish." Give your egg to a special friend.

Students should use the symbols above to decorate their egg.

Page 109

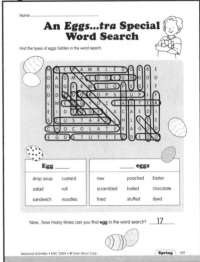

An Eggs...tra Special Word Search

Find the types of eggs hidden in the word search.

Egg _____	_____ eggs
drop soup custard	raw poached Easter
salad roll	scrambled boiled chocolate
sandwich noodles	fried stuffed dyed

Now...how many times can you find **egg** in the word search? ___17___

Page 110

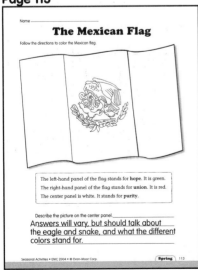

Easter Rabbit Riddles

Count by 6s and then use the code to solve the riddles.

a	6	g	36	m	66	s	90
b	12	h	42	n	72	t	96
c	18	i	48	o	78	u	102
d	24	k	54	r	84	y	108
e	30	l	60				

Why did the Easter Rabbit cross the road?

t h e   c h i c k e n
96 42 30   18 42 48 18 54 30 72

h a d   h i s
42 6 24   42 48 90

e a s t e r   e g g s
30 6 90 96 30 84   30 36 36 90

What is the best way to send a letter to the Easter Rabbit?

b y   h a i r   m a i l
12 108   42 6 48 84   66 6 48 60

What do you get if you pour hot water down the Easter Rabbit's hole?

a   h o t   c r o s s
6   42 78 96   18 84 78 90 90

b u n n y
12 102 72 72 108

Page 111

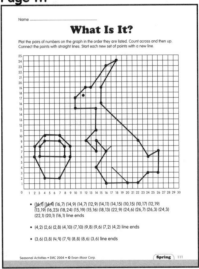

What Is It?

Plot the pairs of numbers on the graph in the order they are listed. Count across and then up. Connect the points with straight lines. Start each new set of points with a new line.

- (16,1) (16,4) (16,7) (14,9) (14,7) (12,9) (14,11) (14,15) (10,15) (10,17) (12,19) (13,19) (16,23) (18,24) (15,19) (15,16) (18,13) (23,19) (24,6) (26,7) (26,3) (24,3) (22,1) (20,1) (16,1) line ends
- (4,2) (2,8) (4,10) (7,10) (9,8) (9,6) (7,2) (4,2) line ends
- (3,6) (3,8) (4,9) (7,9) (8,8) (8,6) (3,6) line ends

Page 112

Cinco de Mayo

Read about Cinco de Mayo and then answer the questions.

Cinco de Mayo means the "fifth of May." It is an important holiday in Mexico. It celebrates the victory of a group of Mexicans over invading French soldiers at the battle of Puebla on May 5, 1862. Cinco de Mayo is a day to remember the courage of those Mexican peasants.

The celebration of Cinco de Mayo includes parades, mock battles, dances, fireworks, and flower festivals. Many Mexican people living in the United States also celebrate this holiday.

1. What is the meaning of Cinco de Mayo? _It means the fifth of May._

2. Why was the battle of Puebla fought? _to gain independence from the invading French soldiers_

3. Does your family celebrate Cinco de Mayo? _Answers will vary._
   If yes, how do you celebrate? _Answers will vary._

Page 113

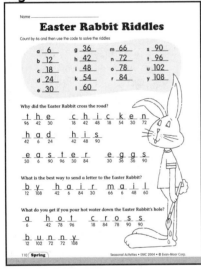

The Mexican Flag

Follow the directions to color the Mexican flag.

The left-hand panel of the flag stands for **hope**. It is green.
The right-hand panel of the flag stands for **union**. It is red.
The center panel is white. It stands for **purity**.

Describe the picture on the center panel.
Answers will vary, but should talk about the eagle and snake, and what the different colors stand for.

Page 114

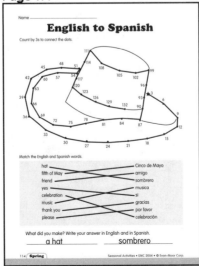

English to Spanish

Count by 3s to connect the dots.

Match the English and Spanish words.

hat	Cinco de Mayo
fifth of May	amigo
friend	sombrero
yes	música
celebration	sí
music	gracias
thank you	por favor
please	celebración

What did you make? Write your answer in English and in Spanish.
a hat   sombrero

Page 117

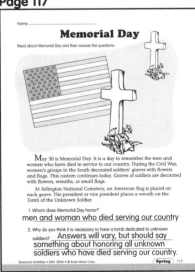

Memorial Day

Read about Memorial Day and then answer the questions.

May 30 is Memorial Day. It is a day to remember the men and women who have died in service to our country. During the Civil War, women's groups in the South decorated soldiers' graves with flowers and flags. This custom continues today. Graves of soldiers are decorated with flowers, wreaths, or small flags.

At Arlington National Cemetery, an American flag is placed on each grave. The president or vice president places a wreath on the Tomb of the Unknown Soldier.

1. Whom does Memorial Day honor?
men and woman who died serving our country

2. Why do you think it is necessary to have a tomb dedicated to unknown soldiers? Answers will vary, but should say something about honoring all unknown soldiers who have died serving our country.

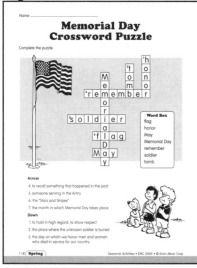

Memorial Day Crossword Puzzle

Complete the puzzle.

Word Box: flag, honor, May, Memorial Day, remember, soldier, tomb

Across
4. to recall something that happened in the past
5. someone serving in the Army
6. the "Stars and Stripes"
7. the month in which Memorial Day takes place

Down
1. to hold in high regard; to show respect
2. the place where the unknown soldier is buried
3. the day on which we honor men and women who died in service for our country

---

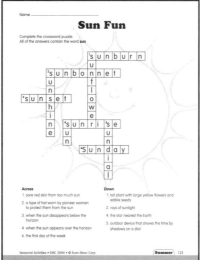

Sun Fun

Complete the crossword puzzle. All of the answers contain the word **sun**.

Across
1. sore red skin from too much sun
2. a type of hat worn by pioneer women to protect them from the sun
3. when the sun disappears below the horizon
4. when the sun appears over the horizon
6. the first day of the week

Down
1. tall plant with large yellow flowers and edible seeds
2. rays of sunlight
4. the star nearest the Earth
5. outdoor device that shows the time by shadows on a dial

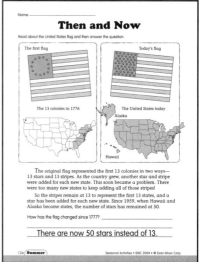

Then and Now

Read about the United States flag and then answer the question.

The first flag — The 13 colonies in 1776
Today's flag — The United States today (Alaska, Hawaii)

The original flag represented the first 13 colonies in two ways—13 stars and 13 stripes. As the country grew, another star and stripe were added for each new state. This soon became a problem. There were too many new states to keep adding all of those stripes!

So the stripes remain at 13 to represent the first 13 states, and a star has been added for each new state. Since 1959, when Hawaii and Alaska became states, the number of stars has remained at 50.

How has the flag changed since 1777?

There are now 50 stars instead of 13.

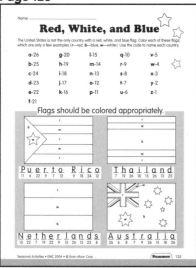

Red, White, and Blue

The United States is not the only country with a red, white, and blue flag. Color each of these flags, which are only a few examples (r—red, b—blue, w—white). Use the code to name each country.

a-26	g-20	l-15	q-10	v-5
b-25	h-19	m-14	r-9	w-4
c-24	i-18	n-13	s-8	x-3
d-23	j-17	o-12	t-7	y-2
e-22	k-16	p-11	u-6	z-1
f-21				

Flags should be colored appropriately.

Puerto Rico — 11 6 22 9 7 12 9 18 24 12
Thailand — 7 19 26 18 15 26 13 23
Netherlands — 13 22 7 19 22 9 15 26 13 23 8
Australia — 26 6 8 7 9 26 15 18 26

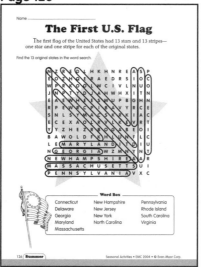

The First U.S. Flag

The first flag of the United States had 13 stars and 13 stripes—one star and one stripe for each of the original states.

Find the 13 original states in the word search.

Word Box
Connecticut, Delaware, Georgia, Maryland, Massachusetts, New Hampshire, New Jersey, New York, North Carolina, Pennsylvania, Rhode Island, South Carolina, Virginia

---

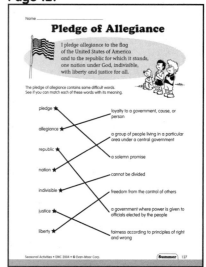

Pledge of Allegiance

I pledge allegiance to the flag of the United States of America and to the republic for which it stands, one nation under God, indivisible, with liberty and justice for all.

The pledge of allegiance contains some difficult words. See if you can match each of these words with its meaning.

- pledge — a solemn promise
- allegiance — loyalty to a government, cause, or person
- republic — a government where power is given to officials elected by the people
- nation — a group of people living in a particular area under a central government
- indivisible — cannot be divided
- justice — fairness according to principles of right and wrong
- liberty — freedom from the control of others

Flag Day

Read about Flag Day and then answer the questions.

Did you know the U.S. flag has two names? It is called the "Stars and Stripes." It is also called "Old Glory." No matter what you call it, the flag stands for the United States of America.

The first U.S. flag had seven red and six white stripes with 13 white stars on a blue background. It became the official U.S. flag on June 14, 1777. Today, June 14 is celebrated as Flag Day with flying flags and patriotic speeches.

1. What are the two nicknames for the U.S. flag?
Old Glory   Stars and Stripes

2. Describe the first U.S. flag.
There were 7 red stripes and 6 white stripes.
There was a blue background with 13 white stars.

Betsy Ross and the 5-Pointed Star

Read about Betsy Ross and then answer the questions.

In 1776, the United States was a new country. It needed a new flag. According to popular legend, George Washington and two other men visited a seamstress named Betsy Ross. They showed her a drawing of the flag they wanted. It had stripes and six-pointed stars. Betsy Ross thought a five-pointed star would look better. She showed the men how easy it was to make one. The men agreed that the five-pointed star should be on the flag.

In June 1977, Congress passed the Flag Resolution, making the "Stars and Stripes" the official flag of the United States.

1. What is the job of a seamstress? to make things by sewing pieces of material together

2. Why did George Washington want a new flag made? The United States was a new country.

3. Circle the star above that you think looks best. Explain your choice. Answers will vary.

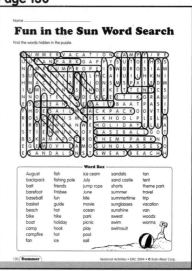

Fun in the Sun Word Search

Find the words hidden in the puzzle.

Word Box
August, backpack, bait, barefoot, baseball, basket, beach, bike, boat, camp, campfire, fan, fish, fishing pole, friends, Frisbee, fun, guide, hat, hike, holiday, hook, ice, ice cream, July, jump rope, June, kite, movie, ocean, park, picnic, play, pool, sail, sandals, sand castle, shorts, summer, summertime, sunglasses, sunshine, sweat, swim, swimsuit, tan, tent, theme park, travel, trip, vacation, van, woods, worms

---

Page 133

Name _____

Sailing, Sailing

Copy the sailboat onto the grid.

Summer winds blowing
White sails billowing
My boat skims over the sea.

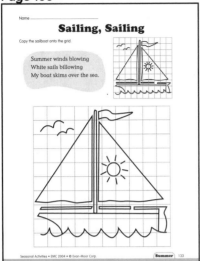

Seasonal Activities • EMC 2004 • © Evan-Moor Corp. | Summer | 133

Page 136

Name _____

Touring North America

Use the code to find the names of these places to visit on vacation.

a-26	g-20	m-14	s-8	w-4
b-25	h-19	n-13	t-7	x-3
c-24	i-18	o-12	u-6	y-2
d-23	j-17	p-11	v-5	z-1
e-22	k-16	q-10		
f-21	r-9			

L a k e   L o u i s e
15 26 16 22   15 12 6 18 8

G r a n d   C a n y o n
20 9 26 13 23   24 26 13 2 12 13

N e w   Y o r k   C i t y
13 22 4   2 12 9 16   24 18 7 2

C a l g a r y
24 26 15 20 26 9 2

R o c k y   M o u n t a i n s
9 12 24 16 2   14 12 6 13 7 26 18 13 8

H a w a i i
19 26 4 26 18 18

W a s h i n g t o n,   D. C.
4 26 8 19 18 13 20 7 12 13   23 24

☞ Choose one place you would like to visit. Explain why on the back of this page.

136 | Summer | Seasonal Activities • EMC 2004 • © Evan-Moor Corp.

Page 138

Name _____

National Parks

In 1872, Yellowstone became the first national park in the United States. It was established to protect the scenic land and to make it available for everyone to visit and enjoy. Today, there are national parks throughout the United States.

Find the national parks hidden in the word search.

Word Box

Badlands	Grand Teton	Rocky Mountain
Big Bend	Haleakala	Saguaro
Bryce Canyon	Lassen	Wind Cave
Canyonlands	Mesa Verde	Yellowstone
Denali	Mount Rainier	Yosemite
Everglades	Olympic	Zion

138 | Summer | Seasonal Activities • EMC 2004 • © Evan-Moor Corp.

Page 139

Name _____

Complete the Face

Draw the other side of this face.

Seasonal Activities • EMC 2004 • © Evan-Moor Corp. | Summer | 139

Page 142

Name _____

Independence Day USA

Independence Day is the greatest patriotic holiday in the United States. It is celebrated on the fourth of July, the day on which the Second Continental Congress signed the Declaration of Independence in 1776. The Declaration was read to the public in Philadelphia four days later and celebrated with ringing bells. Each year all across the United States, we celebrate July 4th with parades, picnics, band concerts, speeches, and fireworks.

Complete the crossword puzzle.

142 | Summer | Seasonal Activities • EMC 2004 • © Evan-Moor Corp.

Page 144

Name _____

Symbols of the USA

Unscramble these names of symbols of the United States of America. Then draw a line to match each word to the correct symbol.

L i b e r t y
B e l l
bertyli lelb

f l a g
agfl

b a l d
e a g l e
dalb geael

S t a t u e   o f
L i b e r t y
tatues fo tyberli

G r e a t   S e a l
eatgr leas

W h i t e
H o u s e
hiwte eoush

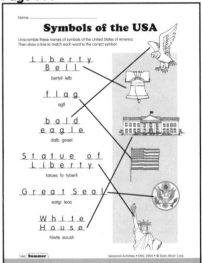

144 | Summer | Seasonal Activities • EMC 2004 • © Evan-Moor Corp.

Page 145

Name _____

Take a Close Look

Find ten differences between the Statues of Liberty.

1. # of points on crown
2. # squares on crown
3. circle on book
4. squares on pedestal
5. facial expression
6. folds on robe
7. hair is different
8. direction of flame
9. bottom of torch
10. colored fingernails

Seasonal Activities • EMC 2004 • © Evan-Moor Corp. | Summer | 145

Page 146

Name _____

The Great Seal of the USA

Read about the Great Seal and then answer the questions.

The Great Seal of the United States was created to serve as an emblem for the United States.

In the center of the seal is our national bird, the bald eagle. The eagle holds a scroll in its beak. The scroll says "e pluribus unum." This means "out of many, one." It shows that we are one nation that was created from many colonies. The Great Seal has many ways of representing the first 13 states:

13 stars above the eagle's head
13 stripes on the shield
13 arrows in the eagle's left claw
13 olives and leaves in the eagle's right claw

The Great Seal is on display in Washington, D.C. It is also on the back of the one-dollar bill.

1. What does "out of many, one" mean? _We are all united._

2. Why are there so many thirteens on the Great Seal? _Because there were thirteen original colonies._

3. If you were designing a seal for the United States, what would you have included? _Answers will vary._

146 | Summer | Seasonal Activities • EMC 2004 • © Evan-Moor Corp.

Notes

_____

_____

_____

_____

_____

_____

_____

_____

_____

_____

_____

_____

_____

_____

_____

_____

Notes